CONTEMPORARY
CLASSICAL ARCHITECTURE
JOHN B. MURRAY

CONTEMPORARY CLASSICAL ARCHITECTURE
JOHN B. MURRAY

Written by Elizabeth Heilman Brooke Murray
Foreword by Bunny Williams
Analytique drawings by Stephen Piersanti

THE MONACELLI PRESS

CONTENTS

FOREWORD

What a thrill it is for me to be invited to write the foreword for the new monograph of John Murray's work. I first met John more than thirty-five years ago, when this young man joined the architectural studio of Parish-Hadley where I was a designer. From the beginning, his talent was obvious. His classically trained eye, his creativity, his attention to detail inspired everyone.

Now to see this new body of work published in this beautiful book is another accolade to his very successful career. Whether John is restoring an old house, redesigning an awkward apartment, or creating a house from the ground up, one always has the sense that this is the way it should have always been. His work has the subtle quality of a master who knows how to design spaces that will stand the test of time. Whether his projects are traditionally inspired or more contemporary, there is always the same attention to detail that makes each space intriguing and memorable. John is not only a very talented architect but also a lovely man whom I am so lucky to have as a dear friend.

Bunny Williams

INTRODUCTION

Turn the pages, look closely. Herein, yes, classical, yet original ideas. Architecture lives, and the stories behind these houses and apartments are meant to be told and read and studied. One client's vision may inspire yours.

Someone once said that architecture is a profession of wise souls. Why is that? Because, as architects, we bring our years of experience and marry them with the fresh dreams of our clients. It is that experience that informs the process as a valuable touchstone for our clients' inspiration. We bring knowledge and skills. They bring visions not yet realized.

The design process in creating architecture is indeed a process. It starts with listening carefully to understand what the design program is and what we must accomplish architecturally. We study the context, determine the limits or constraints. We begin to develop design alternatives, while putting together a successful team of consultants, artisans, craftspeople, suppliers, vendors, always mindful of the necessity of working within our clients' budgets and specific time frames. We coordinate and collaborate with decorators and landscape architects. We compose the design, initially schematically, small scale, and eventually at a scale that can be thought of as full size, with nothing left to the imagination of the builder.

It is in client conversations about what they want to do in a space, how they imagine moving in the space, what elements appeal or charm or calm that architecture begins to take shape. In the design process, we raise a lot of questions. My team and I learn much about the personality of our clients. Do they like to read? Do they like to cook? Do they like to be outdoors? Do they prefer a cozy room? A room bathed in light? What colors feel right to them? Do they like stone? Natural wood?

Inspiration for architectural design is very much about a client's spirit and character, an expression of personal interests, taste, and an awareness that it is in the details that a room will feel right and appropriate. That is where originality and individuality are born.

Best practice architecture is about finding the balance, knowing when to push, when to pull, ensuring an attention to quality in the architecture that supports the decorative vision and makes sense with the clients' furnishings and interior design scheme. More is not always more. We pull all elements together and, like a master chef conceiving and cooking a fine meal, we acknowledge that to make the plan digestible as well as delicious, we do not want to over-season. We are present to know when to show restraint.

A lot of the process is problem-solving, considering how to approach an issue. Sometimes the problems seem almost insurmountable; at a minimum, they require handling complex situations. The exciting part for me is coming up with that sometimes unexpected design solution, distilling all the criteria presented and achieving a design concept that not only is highly functional but also has a quality of beauty, sense of proportion and of appropriateness. Ideally design solutions support the concept of having it all: they celebrate the view, bathe the interior in natural light, accomplish the functional needs successfully—be they storage or display or comfort.

Yes, a classical perspective shows an appreciation for the artistry of the past or the classic simplicity of the forms, but the projects herein show that layers of classical architectural framing and complex problem-solving are for the here and the now. In Beaux-Arts parlance, I particularly like the coming together of the *parti,* or the essence, of the architectural plan, the clarity of the organization, the compositional hierarchy of the spaces, the proportions, the scale, the articulation of the spaces, the rooms.

It is realizing the big idea of any given project that I personally most relish, and for this reason analytique drawings are created during the design phase of all of our projects. The analytique gives us an opportunity to pull back and recognize the strong compositional qualities on a variety of scales. The analytique often speaks to the overall plan, section, elevation, and it also pulls the scale up to the actual shape-making of the project's defining elements, a cornice, a stair balustrade, a mantel detail.

As architects, we bring to our projects an openness to seeing how solutions to specific site constraints can be forward thinking in terms of technology and the latest modern conveniences. Our architectural residences have the potential to be around for a very long time. That potential longevity instills in us a responsibility to get it right, to assure that it sits comfortably on the site, that it is built to last. Yes, the architectural projects here are of a time and a place, but what will always set them apart are the original, yet still classic details that connect them to the timeless innovators of the past, the inventors of the present, the visionaries of the future.   *John B. Murray*

ODE TO CENTRAL PARK

Urban archaeology. We are becoming known for our dexterity and ingenuity in making two apartments one with a stunning statement of a staircase. In this case, there were actually three apartments in an architectural icon on Central Park South designed in 1926 by A. Rollin Caughey and William F. Evans Jr. and completed in 1938. Because of the Depression, the building was constructed in fits and starts, depending on available funding.

We have taken many estate-condition apartments back to the bare systems in order to construct the vision of our clients, but in this instance, it was extremely complicated. And that was where the unexpected urban archaeology "presented" itself. As we prepared for construction, we learned that the lower floor must, at some point in the building's history, been the very top floor. What did that mean? It meant that mechanical and plumbing systems were housed horizontally, which clearly was not in keeping with the vertical vision. With some patience and much team problem-solving, numerous hurdles and challenges were navigated to allow us to execute our clients' vision.

Their concept for this New York City aerie was multilayered, rich in detail, always artistically considered. Within the horizontal and vertical 5,000 square feet of interior space, we were asked to establish a private suite for the owners as well as a graceful floor plan for entertaining family, friends, business colleagues. With a generously sized gallery, natural rift-cut oak library, study, and bar as well as the master bedroom suite, the lower floor can be a private enclave, or a space ready for the transition from office mandates to the business of serving as host. The library is warm and comfortable with deep honey-finished custom millwork. Flanking the hearth, the two paired Harmon hinge doors to the master suite have a refined design that, when closed, meet our clients' request for privacy, yet, when open, permit an easy flow from the master bedroom to the library, which can serve as a sitting room.

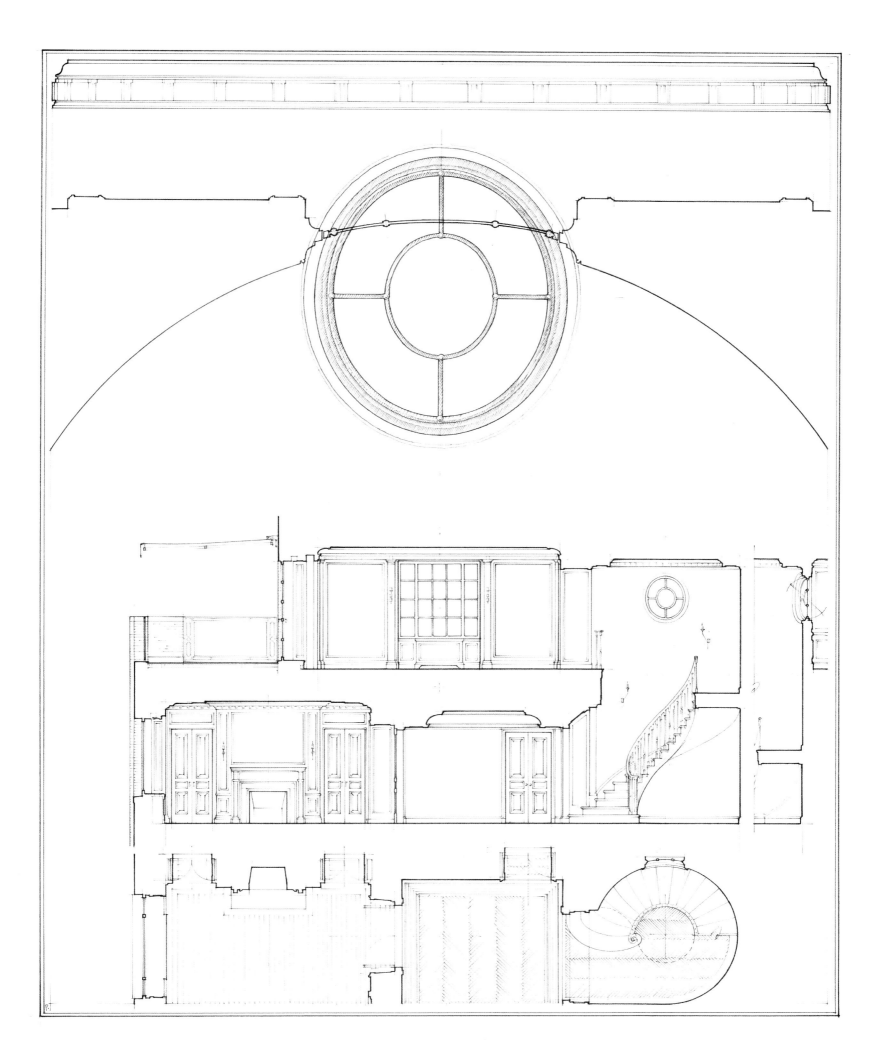

LOWER FLOOR

UPPER FLOOR

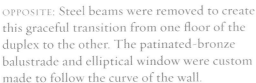

OPPOSITE: Steel beams were removed to create this graceful transition from one floor of the duplex to the other. The patinated-bronze balustrade and elliptical window were custom made to follow the curve of the wall.

We are known for the design and installation of truly memorable staircases, but the unique history of this building posed unusual challenges. To make the vertical connection and install the staircase, we were forced to reconfigure a web of steel girders and beams. Then the magic of client and team creativity took place. The compositional genius was finding solutions to make a staircase that is remarkably gracious in scale, shape, and form and also works with the bones of the building. The staircase now serves as a strong interconnection of space as well as a very artful element with a play of curving stair stringer and bronze balustrade designed to flow with the elliptical curve of the wall. In order to draw light from an east-facing window into the stair hall and give the family room a truly unique central focal point, we designed an operable, bowed oval window in handblown glass with a patinated-bronze frame. Constructed as a complex curve, it follows the curvature of the stair hall wall and provides a distinctive visual connection as well as a series of thought-provoking internal views.

The Central Park views from this apartment are poetically breathtaking. How gratifying it was to work with our clients to transform a rotting, water-damaged terrace and balustrade into a lovely space with a basket-weave patterned stone floor! We inserted two sets of bronze French doors and a custom-designed glass-and-bronze balustrade to acknowledge the gift of the enchanting views. Our clients were so inspired by the luxurious greensward at their doorstep that they and interior designer Tammy Connor asked muralist Scott Waterman to paint intimate Central Park views to wrap around the lower gallery and up the staircase. Recognized with a Stanford White award, the finished architecture and art statement here is indeed a visual ode to Central Park.

ABOVE: Harmon hinge doors of rift-cut white oak permit an ease of movement from the gallery into the master suite but also afford needed privacy. OPPOSITE: Light from Central Park glances across the library and into the gallery. The deep plaster cornice, while concealing building mechanical systems, adds an intimacy to the gallery. Bucolic scenes of the park are captured on the mural that wraps the gallery and extends up the stair.

OPPOSITE: Steps up from the library to his study make working at home an easy commute. Custom-designed bookshelves and paneling are of a warm, antiqued and waxed white oak. ABOVE: Harmon hinge doors flanking the fireplace lead to the master suite. FAR RIGHT: The custom mantel complements the paneling of the room. RIGHT: The bar is just steps from his study, cleverly placed for an easy transition to the business of hosting.

RIGHT: Plaster cornice and ceiling panels, herringbone wood floors, and new bronze French doors leading to the terrace lend a fresh elegance to the living room. OVERLEAF LEFT: Painted pocket doors slide closed to keep the family room and kitchen from view. OVERLEAF RIGHT: Match-strike frieze articulation, a paneled ceiling, and pilasters complement contemporary furniture and sconces.

OPPOSITE: New bronze fenestration provides the latest technology in insulation and soundproofing. The shallow paneling of the coved ceiling conceals air-conditioning supply vents. ABOVE: With a glass-and-bronze balustrade and new stone paving, the terrace was completely refreshed to become one of Manhattan's most extraordinary outdoor rooms.

LEFT: Light from Central Park casts across the living room into the second-floor stair hall, while the elliptical window adds light from the family room. ABOVE: A specially blended blue lacquer paint brings warmth to the family room and visually connects it to the adjoining kitchen.

RIGHT: The range hood with brass strapping and pot rail, custom-designed to complement the French range, anchors the room on the central wall textured with Calacatta Gold marble tiles. The pop-up in the ceiling over the island maximizes height and conceals mechanical grilles.

ABOVE: Oh, what a beautiful morning! The expansive window and window seat are designed for savoring the Central Park view throughout the day. OPPOSITE: Mirrors enhance natural light in the master bath, which features a twin-sink stand and an etched-glass shower door.

CLASSIC GLAMOUR

Trust the process. It is in the conversations about the past and walks through the space in the present that each client's aesthetic becomes apparent, and sometimes their artistic eye evolves, as, week by week, we map out the program and hone in on the details. In this case we began with a setting of drama and distinction, a limestone-clad Italian Renaissance-style building designed by Emery Roth, overlooking the grand stairs of the Metropolitan Museum of Art and the seasonal delights of Central Park.

Combining two apartments into one full-floor plan to meet the needs of an active family of six was our overarching program. Our depth of experience working with craftsmen who honor the traditional process was vital for meeting the standards of the building. Simple sheetrock walls would not do. To maintain the integrity of the building's infrastructure, new walls required the handiwork of masons and plaster artisans.

When you have a Central Park view, why not flaunt it? By reinventing the apartment's 5,500 square foot floorplan, we were able to bring the light from the Fifth Avenue windows into spaces to be shared. The original master bathroom was transformed into a gracious lace-wood library with dark stained-oak accents. The light-filled living room is now grandly centered between the dining room and the library with pocket doors that can be retracted for freedom of flow or closed for more formal gatherings. An intimate lace-wood bar is now ideally positioned off the entry gallery yet also is an extension of the library.

Working with interior designers Tony Ingrao and Randy Kemper, we were able to make the fireplaces in the dining room and the master bedroom signature focal points in both a public space and a private one. The concave shape of the chimney breasts with a textural custom plaster technique accentuating both chimney breasts exemplify the care we took with all detail. Polished-nickel bespoke Greek key metalwork lends quiet classical dignity to the dining room mantel, the yin to the yang, the glamour of the custom-designed light fixture over the dining table.

Listening to and adding layers of materials and craftsmanship to our clients' creative vision not only permitted us to watch their ideas about their living space evolve, but also afforded us unexpected opportunities to contrast classical vocabulary with contemporary verve. What began as a new entry door became a striking work of art, crafted of a unique translucent art glass that admits light into the entry but maintains an element of privacy at the same time. Set into a black marble casing, the custom metalwork of the door

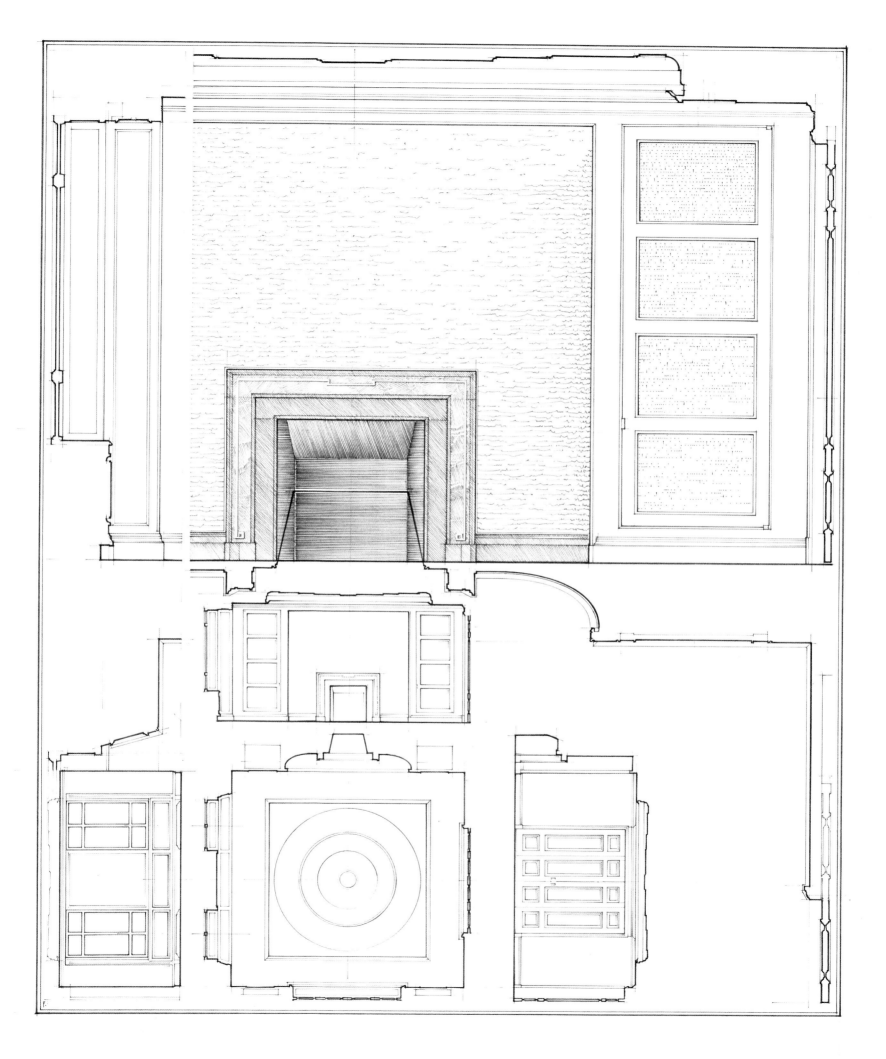

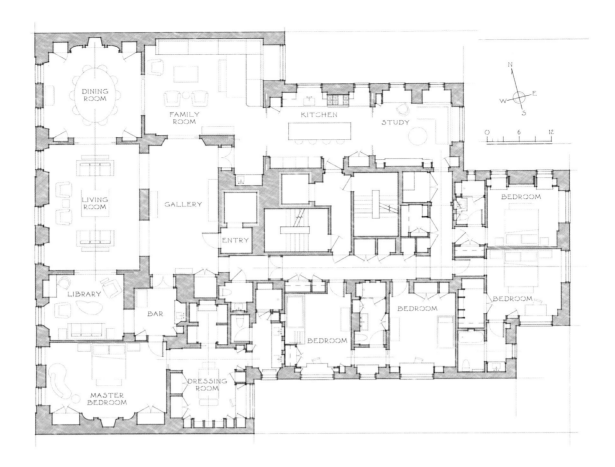

was fabricated by classically trained metal craftsmen.

The corridor leading to additional family bedrooms features impressive detail in the polished lacquer finish mahogany doors and multilayered plaster cornices. It is a hallway of many doors—doors leading to the family's private world and others hidden, jib doors concealing precious New York City storage space.

As we designed the family room to comfortably open to the kitchen, we discussed how doors might slide open or close for entertaining, and we learned that father and sons enjoyed solving math and physics proofs together. We heard and were able to deliver a pocketing floor-to-ceiling white board for erasable problem-solving! This is, indeed, something that truly makes the family's space uniquely theirs.

As paintings and sculpture were found and came to influence the selection of materials and interior design, we were pleased to realize that we had provided the traditional shapes and canvas for the rich textures and modern materials that define this new home as extraordinarily current and lasting.

PRECEDING SPREAD: Layers of refined classical detail in the coved ceiling, ornamental plaster cornice, nickel-banded black marble door jambs, casings, and baseboard are enhanced by the polished white marble floor with black marble and nickel woven banding. OPPOSITE: The reflective entry door of nickel, bronze and wrought iron complements its black marble frame.

OPPOSITE: The coved ceilings in the living room conceal an awkward central beam and lighting and air conditioning around the perimeter. Pocket doors close to make the library a more intimate space or slide open for entertaining. Black marble thresholds with nickel accent bands open to the gallery.

ABOVE: Classically custom, the powder room features a reed-articulated cornice and a polished-nickel vanity with fluted pilasters. OPPOSITE: In the dining room, concentric disks in pearlescent silver leaf are a foil to the sparkle of the faceted-glass ribbon chandelier. A unique plaster technique accentuates the fireplace niche, which is flanked by china cabinets executed in art glass and polished-nickel trim.

PRECEDING SPREAD LEFT:
A view from the kitchen
through open pocket doors
to the living room and
dining room windows
overlooking Fifth Avenue.
PRECEDING SPREAD
RIGHT: The light-filled living
room is now centered
between the dining room
and the library. RIGHT: The
family room also serves as
an informal dining area.
Continuous art lighting is
concealed in the ceiling.

PRECEDING SPREAD LEFT: The original master bathroom was transformed into a lace-wood library with ebonized oak accents.
PRECEDING SPREAD RIGHT: A paneled wall of the bar conceals the door to the master bedroom. One of the pilasters flanking the built-in shelves and cabinet conceals a wine closet. ABOVE: With a curved niche, textured walls and flanking closets with art glass and nickel-trimmed doors, the master bedroom fireplace mimics that of the dining room.
OPPOSITE: Her dressing room is wrapped in custom cabinetry with textured leather panels and glass transoms that illuminate.

ALL ABOUT FAMILY

It takes courage to expand a vision and commit to making an existing property truly one's own. When we were introduced to our clients, they had just purchased a "Hamptons getaway" on two acres in East Hampton overlooking a fifty-acre nature preserve. The house was fifty percent constructed, but the design did not consider the needs of the young, active family about to take ownership. Our project became an extensive redesign with selective removals and additions. The overriding theme was all about family.

We were asked to dig deeper, expand, enhance, improve, maintain the character of the shingle style architecture, while configuring rooms that sensibly connect for casual living indoors and out and provide space for extended family and friends. To imprint what became a more than 16,000-square-foot house with distinctive touches that particularly appeal to our clients, we reconfigured fenestration and doors and integrated a very refined custom articulation of corbeling and bracketing on both the exterior and interior to evoke the nineteenth-century cottages on Long Island.

Creating spaces that capture views is an important element of all our projects. Here we added a dining porch for savoring the nature preserve and swimming pool views. We designed a pool with a pergola-covered seating area, an outdoor shower, a changing room, and a small kitchen.

We redesigned the entry hall and stair with boarded trayed ceilings that soar to more than twenty feet. Light now streams in from second-story windows. With interior designer Victoria Hagan, we custom-designed a cushioned bench that is now a ready spot for welcoming guests or resting a bag.

Since modern-day living takes place in the kitchen, the more casual dining room, and the family room, we opened up the core of the house and its floor plan to improve movement from family room to kitchen. We added all new inswing and pocketing French doors, scaling up the glass pane sizes to create a more expansive interior ambience.

Arguably the most beloved room of the house, any house, the screened dining porch was designed with heated basket-weave bluestone floors that extend into the mudroom. There is a coffered ceiling and seating for fourteen. From autumn through spring screens can be removed and replaced with glass windows for a precious greenhouse feel.

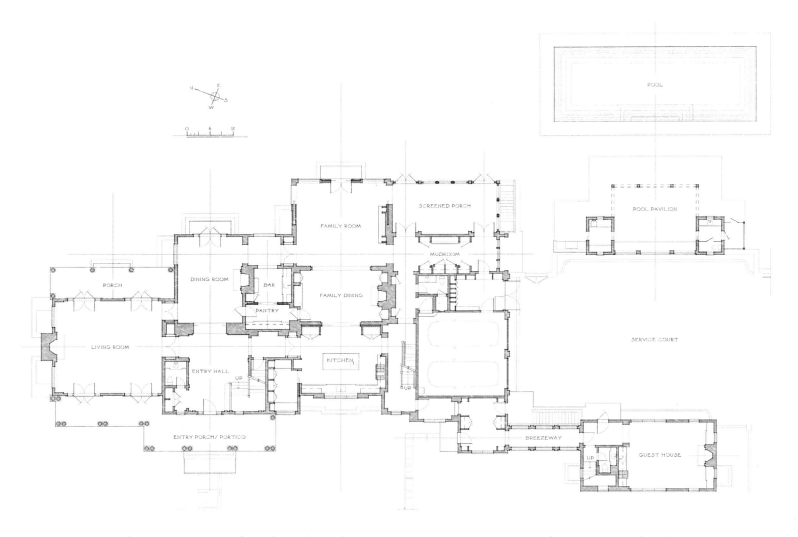

A guesthouse connected with a glassed-in breezeway was just one of a number of additions to the property. We established a more gracious motor court entry that leads to a new service court, and from there to a pragmatic mudroom, which includes a built-in bench with pegs for hanging coats, bags, hats and storage for sports equipment. We excavated the basement as a comprehensive lower level with high ceilings, adding a kitchenette, a fun bunk room for sleeping six, and locker-like bathrooms.

We put in a sunken US Open-sized Har-Tru tennis court with a high wainscot of horizontal cedar boarding and a pergola-shaded viewing stand. By sinking the court, the surrounding privet hedge does not need to extend above six feet in height.

Now in nearly every season this family compound is a personally distinctive retreat for swimming or tennis or, in peaceful splendor, sharing stillness with white-tailed deer, red foxes, and barn swallows.

PRECEDING SPREAD: The rear elevation evokes the form and detailing of nineteenth-century shingled cottages, with twin projecting gambrel facades, eyebrow dormers, and cottage-style windows. OPPOSITE: Shaped brackets extend from the family room with twelve-over-one windows. Above the lead-coated flashing and gutter is a crafted-patterned wood balustrade braced between paneled piers. Shaped brackets support the pediment of the gambrel facade.

OPPOSITE: We redesigned the entry hall and stair with boarded trayed ceilings that soar to twenty feet. Light now streams in from re-spaced second-story windows. A strategic expansion of the building footprint made possible the addition of the powder room vestibule off the entry hall. ABOVE: A cushioned bench is a welcoming addition to the entry hall. OVERLEAF: The living room is the full width of the house, opening to porches front and back. It features a coffered v-groove boarded ceiling and a bolection mantel with a bracketed shelf.

OPPOSITE: The primary entrance from the motor court is now the mud room, with a built-in bench, pegs, and closets for storing rackets, hats, and helmets. The bluestone floor is set in a basket weave pattern. ABOVE: With new inswing, French doors, concealed pocketing screen doors, and flanking windows, the family room is all about the view.

RIGHT: An inviting, spacious kitchen with a boarded coffered ceiling and white oak plank flooring features an island with drawers and turned legs that evoke a traditional farm table. The integrated upper cabinets are supported on shaped wood brackets. Oil-rubbed bronze hardware dramatically accents the cabinets. The deep-paneled doorway leads to the secondary stair hall.

OPPOSITE: As seen from the upper landing defined by the balustrade and wainscot, the entry hall is capped by a boarded, paneled trayed ceiling. ABOVE: The addition of a wood-burning fireplace and a plush window seat makes a cozy master bedroom. The illusion of an even more expansive space was achieved by raising the ceiling to follow the pitch of the roof.

RIGHT: The dining porch, articulated with pilasters supporting a high-beamed ceiling with boarding, has openings with screens that can be interchanged with glass sashes for use in all seasons. The radiant-heated bluestone floors also ensure year-round comfort.

ABOVE: The sunken tennis court is lined with shiplap cedar boarding. The viewing stand, shaded by a pergola, consists of untreated cedar purlins and slats supported by painted cedar posts and beams. OPPOSITE: The pool pergola is flanked by a changing room and a kitchenette with oculus windows. Fixed louvers in untreated cedar above a long continuous bench allow cross-ventilation while visually concealing the service court and guest house.

THOUGHTFULLY ARTISTIC

I n a 1911 building acknowledged as an Arts and Crafts masterpiece, our clients started with a 6,200-square-foot duplex overlooking Central Park. From many of the main rooms, it truly feels as if the park is right there, the always-changing trees just beyond reach. In initial meetings, our clients referenced the spirit and simplicity of a New England church interior with light washing walls and asked us to maximize the effect of natural light and enhance views.

Arts and Crafts buildings are rare in New York City, and this one, designed by Henry Wilhelm Wilkinson, has the distinction of having been built to provide studios for artists and actors. Our client herself is a painter and sculptor whose eye for color and design is exacting. An element of our program was to provide her with a painting studio with homosote walls for pinning up sketches of ideas-in-the-making.

The creative tour de force of this apartment, and greatest challenge, was rethinking and reconstructing the connection between the two floors. We were presented with such a small spiral staircase that the two levels felt disengaged with no sense of flow between them. This was remedied by carving out the core of the apartment and completely reimagining the stair hall as a majestic, two-story volume. Upstairs, an interior dressing room and closets were cleared to make way for a client-inspired stained-oak billiard room with built-in bookshelves that met a variety of program requests. Thanks to French doors leading into the family room, light is brought in across the apartment from Central Park. On the first floor, there is now a sumptuous gallery with a theatrically dramatic staircase.

To add gravitas to the gallery, we collaborated with interior designer Stephen Sills and craftsmen to layer and texture plastering in the central stair hall. The living room also features plaster paneling and a coffered ceiling, a thoughtful design maneuver to work with an existing beam. A patterned frieze was inspired by the building's Arts and Crafts heritage. Our clients requested custom-designed bronze-lined firewood storage in both the living room and the family room so the light of fire can easily dance in these rooms.

By New York City standards, we created an opulently spacious kitchen and breakfast room with custom painted cabinetry, burnished brass hardware, a comfortable banquette, a built-in desk, and Carrara marble countertops and backsplash.

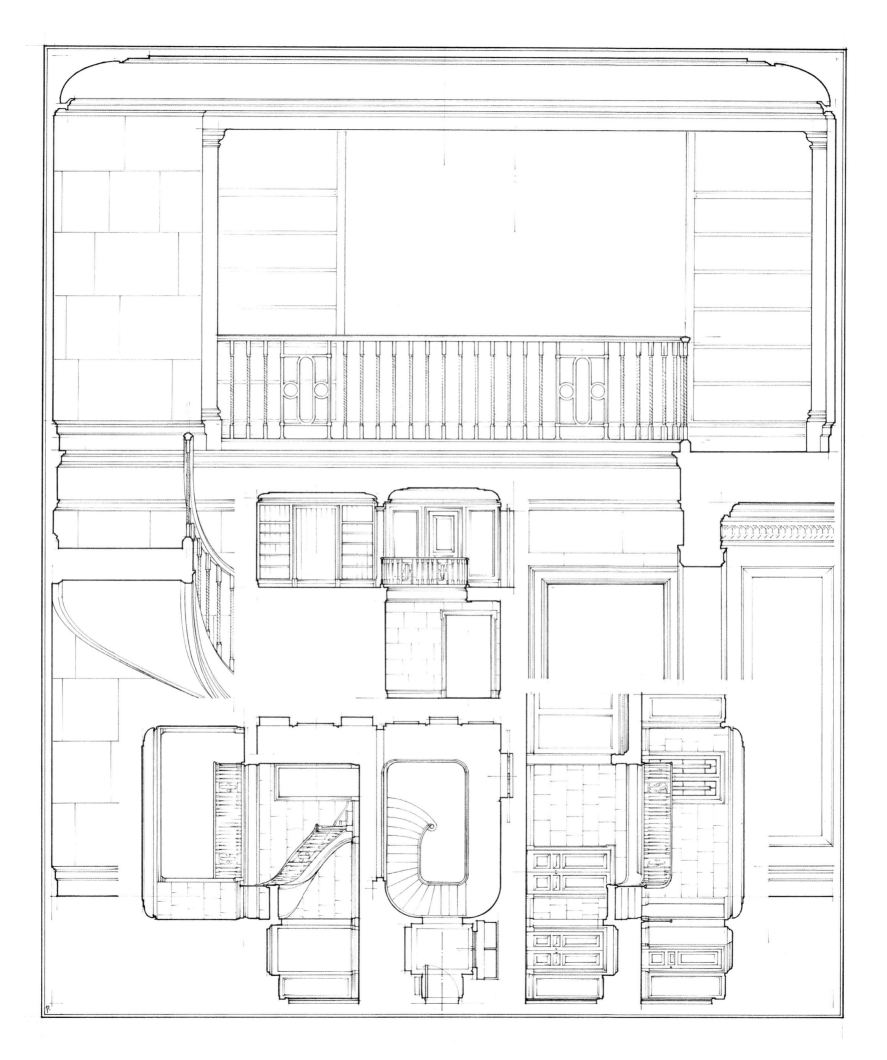

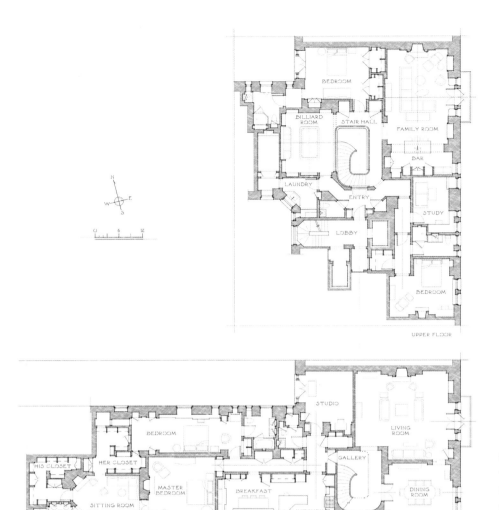

UPPER FLOOR

LOWER FLOOR

OPPOSITE: The apartment was made up of multiple smaller units on two adjoining floors with a narrow spiral stair that did not encourage movement. A more gracious floor plan was achieved by carving out the entry space and creating a sweeping staircase within a grander gallery.

Working very closely with the Landmarks Preservation Commission to adhere to strict requirements for valence, hardware, and color, we replaced the awnings on the terraces overlooking the park. We replaced all the French doors and windows with counterweighted insulated glass and painted mahogany frames and sashes. In the major rooms facing the park, we added mirrors to the side jambs to reflect more light and capture unexpected views.

Family gatherings, sharing time with family and friends, is important to our clients. With a working fireplace, beamed ceiling, wet bar with copper sink and fittings, a banquette, and French doors flanked by double-hung sidelights opening to a terrace, the family room has become an entertaining space—not to mention a coveted spot for viewing the joyous floats and balloons of the Thanksgiving Day Parade.

RIGHT: The coffered ceiling in the living room integrates a patterned plaster frieze. The patinated-bronze niche for the firewood echoes the surround of the custom marble fireplace. Mirrored side jambs expand the French doors with double-hung sidelights leading to the balcony.

PRECEDING SPREAD LEFT: A walnut pocket door with a unique pyramidal lock panel permits a painterly view from living room to dining room. PRECEDING SPREAD RIGHT: Parquet de Versailles floors connect the dining room, living room, and gallery. Light from Central Park now streams across the dining room into the gallery. ABOVE AND OPPOSITE: The cabinetry in the kitchen and breakfast room is custom designed with restoration glass. Countertops and backsplashes are Carrara marble; the wood cutting board inset next to the sink and the farm table are both custom designs.

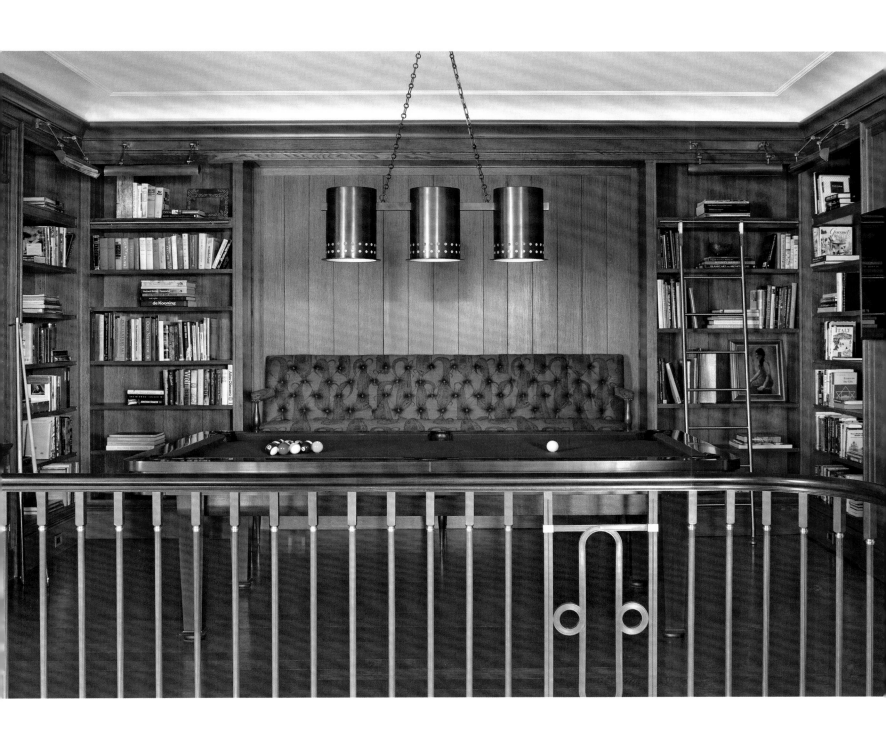

OPPOSITE AND ABOVE: At the top of the stairs, a dressing room and closets were reconfigured as a stained-oak billiard room with a coved ceiling and custom bookshelves that form a niche for the owners' billiard bench. The dark patinated-bronze balustrade with polished mahogany hand rail frames the monumental opening to the stair hall.

ABOVE: The central alcove of the family room is fabricated of oak with French doors flanked by double-hung sidelights and mirrored side panels that open to an awninged balcony. Twin inset bookcases provide storage for treasured family volumes as well as firewood for the working fireplace. OPPOSITE: With oak plank flooring, counter seating, and a banquette by the window, the bar opens to the family room.

RIGHT: The bay window alcove in the master bedroom is articulated with custom wood paneling. A former walk-in closet became a sitting room connecting the master bedroom to the master bath. The passage is framed with Harmon hinged doors.

RIGHT: His and her walk-in closets are hidden off this luxurious sitting room. The unique pyramidal shape of the lock panel of the doors is a signature feature of the apartment.

A Grand Entrance

When world travels provide inspiration, it takes a sophisticated eye and sensibility to take a good idea and pare it down for the space available in a Manhattan pied-à-terre. In this instance, our clients were influenced by a fondness for British architect Sir Edwin Lutyens and, in particular, Lutyens's design for the entry of the Viceroy's House in New Delhi. Our clients, who are based in California, asked us to transform a 2,750-square-foot apartment in a J. E. R. Carpenter Italian Renaissance–style building on Park Avenue into a flowing floor plan to unite the living room and dining room as a single space for entertaining.

An added dimension to our creative process here was the ease of working in collaboration with interior designer Brian McCarthy. We both trained under the courtly Albert Hadley, a diligent gentleman and resilient solver of problems, who insisted on getting every detail just "right." In this group effort not only did we rely on the exactitude of our early training, but we were blessed to be working with clients who share our passion for pushing artisans to masterful results.

Lutyens was a master of the grand entrance. Our redesign here involved returning the entry from a square room to its original round shape. To establish the gracious center of the apartment, we moved the powder room so that guests enter the rotunda at its center and truly feel they have "arrived." Our aim was to accentuate height along all axes with a shallow dome ceiling and to strike a balance between attention to texture, color, materials, and their ornamental possibilities and the majesty of restraint. The rusticated entry and rotunda walls are finished in an ultra-flat paint enhanced with marble dust; the Lutyens-inspired floor design is a pared-back dance of subtle diamonds, bands, and circles in bianco sheer, Gohara, and basalt black marble. The new powder room features a bianco sheer marble wainscot, lacquered walls, a plaster cornice, and a mesmerizing use of mirror to explode the space.

Each room off the rotunda is framed by a unique pilaster design. What was a dark, wood-paneled dining room now embraces its Central Park view, and, with twice-bleached oak flooring, a high-gloss ceiling, and walls of antiqued watery mirror, celebrates all available light. By maintaining a consistent cornice profile, but with unique capitals in dining room and living room, the rooms appear as one flowing space yet are understood for their unique purposes as well. In the living room, we expressed beams and selected a specific recessed light to maximize ceiling height.

Artisans were challenged to perfection to make ebony-painted three-paneled pyramidal doors throughout and walls of Venetian plaster cuts-outs in the study. In contrast, the custom bookshelves are austere in their simplicity, quietly expressing a keen eye for three dimensions in their reed-carved edges.

ABOVE LEFT AND OPPOSITE: Basalt black, Gohara, and bianco sheer marble create a dramatic floor in the rotunda gallery. Rusticated millwork walls are painted with marble dust for a subtle sparkle. ABOVE RIGHT: A memorable welcome: an entry niche with a custom table design by Brian McCarthy.

RIGHT: Light streams across the Venetian plaster walls of the living room. Reed-and-pearl capitals of the fluted plaster pilasters frame a mosaic mantel at the opening to the alcove and play with the light and the vivid colors in the room.

ABOVE AND OPPOSITE: The L-shaped plan accommodates multiple settings for conversation in the main living room and adjoining alcove. Beams are expressed, and ceilings are finished in a high gloss to maximize the sense of space. The floors are bleached white oak. A subtle articulation in the plaster cornice adds texture and movement to the paneled ceiling.

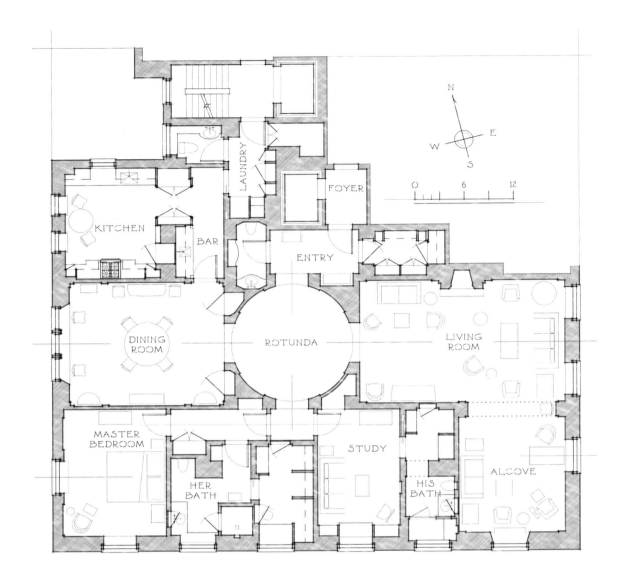

Both his bathroom and her bathroom were configured with adjoining dressing rooms, and they incorporate materials that reflect and magnify natural light: palladium silver leaf and white onyx in her bath, bleached sycamore and crema delicato marble in his.

To provide an eat-in kitchen and one that accommodates for cooking for more than a few, we captured the space of a staff bedroom, reconfigured the windows for a symmetrical balance, and added eight-inch-wide white-oak plank flooring painted in gray and white stripes.

Yes, space has been transformed for entertaining utility, and with an extraordinary architectural and artistic presence.

OPPOSITE, CLOCKWISE FROM LEFT: Three-panel pyramidal doors received a high-gloss lacquered finish for added dimensionality; in the dining room, capitals of stylized acanthus leaves crown the pilasters flanking a mirror; the space of a small bedroom was reconfigured as a connecting bar and larger kitchen; in the powder room, high-gloss black panels are installed over a bianco sheer wainscot, which meets a basalt black and bianco sheer marble floor with nickel banding.

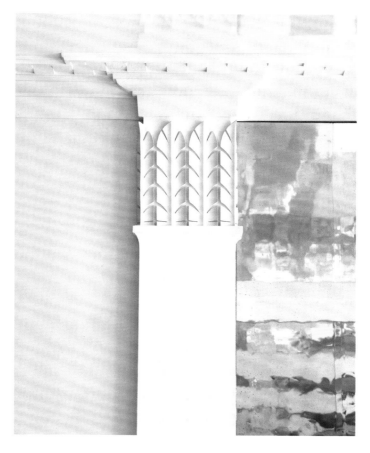

RIGHT: The dining room flows naturally from the rotunda of the apartment. A wall of watery antique mirror and a high-gloss ceiling reflect and enhance all available light. Custom cabinetry on either side of the opening to the rotunda holds silver, glassware, and china. Mirror inset in the door surround is a glamorous touch.

ABOVE LEFT: Inspired by Matisse cutouts, the patterned elements on the walls of
the study are hand-cut and plastered. A pocket door closes off his dressing room and
bath. ABOVE RIGHT: Bleached sycamore and Crema Delicato marble in his bath.
OPPOSITE: In contrast to the lively patterned walls, the custom bookshelves are austere
in their simplicity, quietly expressing three dimensions in their reed-carved edges.

ABOVE: Striated walls, plaster cornices, and high-gloss painted ceilings define the master bedroom. The reflectivity of the ceiling gives the illusion that the room is more expansive than it actually is. Custom cabinetry beneath the window conceals a television and its lift mechanism. RIGHT: In her bath starphire mirror and palladium silver-leaf paneled millwork with a white onyx countertop shimmer in the light.

RIGHT: A La Cornue range and hood in "summer blue" and polished nickel, is complemented by custom cabinets and Calacatta calida marble countertops and backsplash.

Return Reimagine

Among the greatest of professional pleasures is having the opportunity to continue the creative process with clients as they enter a new phase of their lives. In this instance, we had worked with the client about ten years earlier to renovate and make a townhouse "hers." With the passing of time, daughters were off to college; the client had remarried; certain rooms and floors could now reflect the family's new life. We could reconsider how rooms might be configured.

Changes in the first-floor entertaining spaces, the stair hall, family room, kitchen, and breakfast room were more about a fresh interior design. We had worked with Bunny Williams on the original renovation, so there was an ease in the design process that comes from having already listened to a client's preferences and helped to establish a unique aesthetic as well as a generous and trusting collaboration that permits all involved to confidently focus on the details and savor the process—knowing from experience that this team would undoubtedly create spaces that would make us all proud.

During this life transition, we were asked to establish a distinct his bathroom using Botticino stone with accent stone in Corinthian Beige and include a custom-designed vanity and medicine cabinet. Our new program also asked that a former bedroom be transformed into his study with cabinetry for his art and antique collection and a separate, less visible space for office supplies. The new vision dispelled a heavy stalwart feel and added cleaner, lighter coved moldings and cornices. The newly designed study provided wall cabinets that house books, art, and the TV. By removing a wall, we transformed two former children's rooms into a more gracious guest room. Off this bedroom, we added elegance to the terrace by replacing single-pane glass doors with a French door and sidelights.

Returning after ten years of technological advancements meant we could install the latest heating, ventilation, and air-conditioning systems. We were also able to increase the energy efficiency of the existing skylight by using state-of-the-art double-insulated low-E safety glass and installing a fabric solar-shading system.

A key mandate for this return-and-reimagine project was that we take great care to seamlessly blend new design work. So, while we added levels of detail and refinement, we, in some instances, improved a space in a way that appears there was minimal architectural and design intervention. We transformed rooms for new purpose and brought a fresh design for a new phase of life.

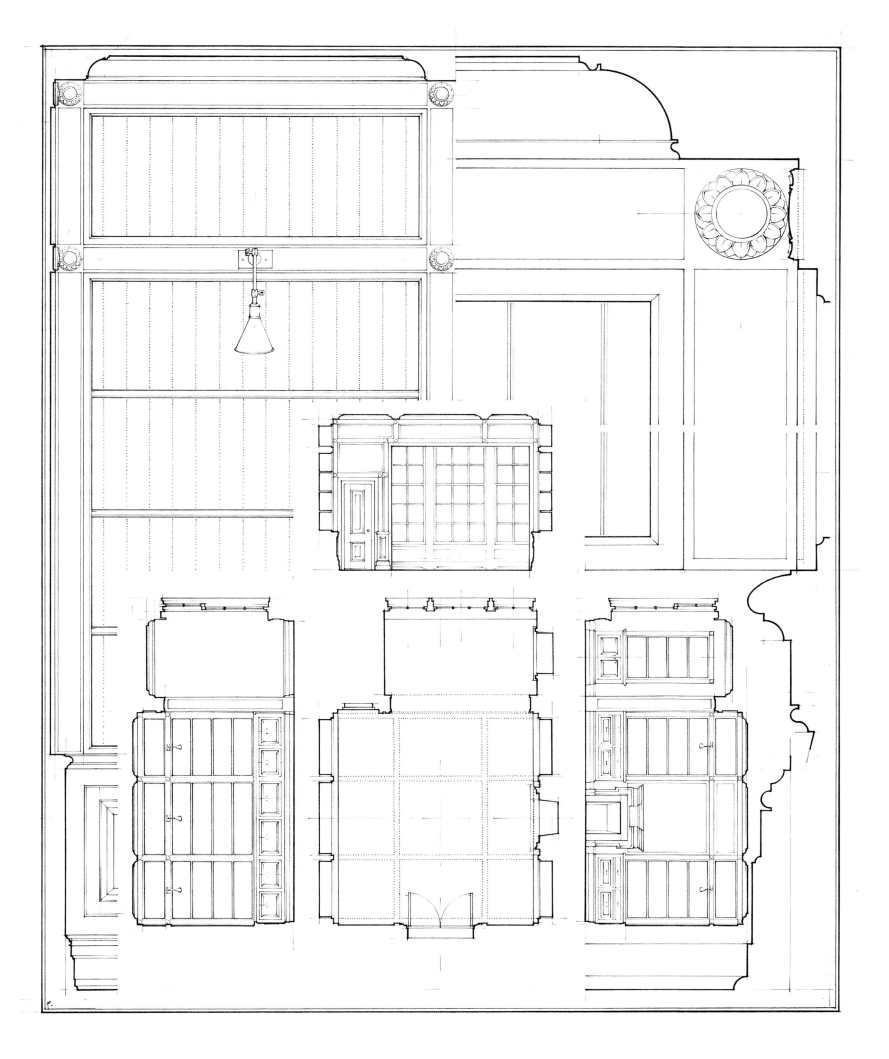

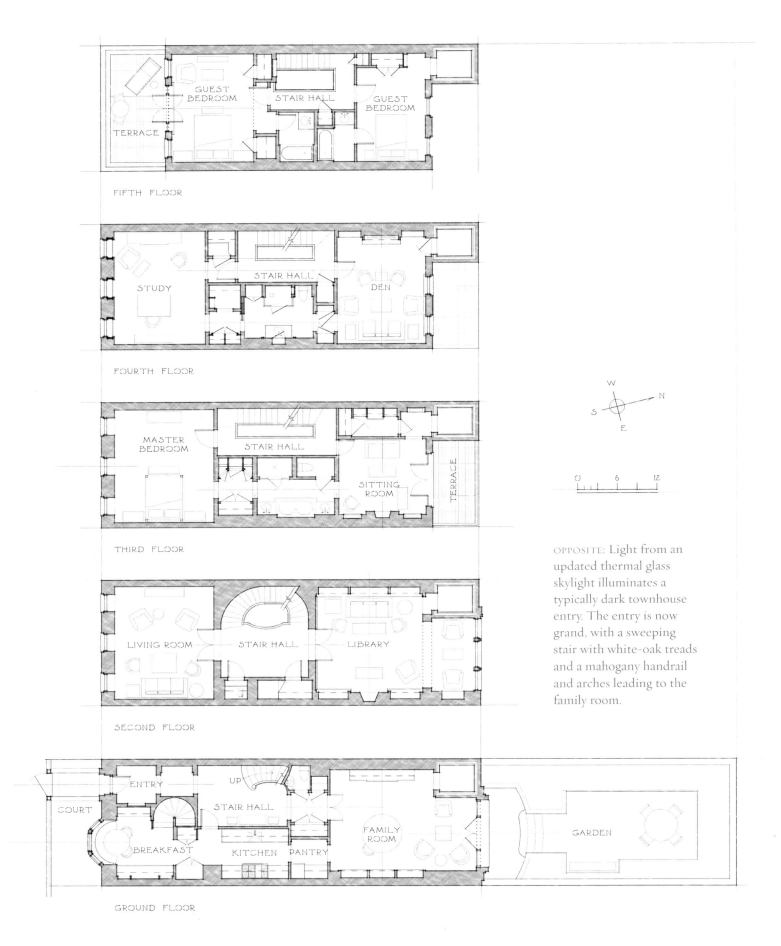

FIFTH FLOOR

TERRACE
GUEST BEDROOM
STAIR HALL
GUEST BEDROOM

FOURTH FLOOR

STUDY
STAIR HALL
DEN

THIRD FLOOR

MASTER BEDROOM
STAIR HALL
SITTING ROOM
TERRACE

W N
S E

0   6   12

SECOND FLOOR

LIVING ROOM
STAIR HALL
LIBRARY

OPPOSITE: Light from an updated thermal glass skylight illuminates a typically dark townhouse entry. The entry is now grand, with a sweeping stair with white-oak treads and a mahogany handrail and arches leading to the family room.

GROUND FLOOR

ENTRY
UP
COURT
STAIR HALL
BREAKFAST
KITCHEN
PANTRY
FAMILY ROOM
GARDEN

ABOVE AND OPPOSITE: A high-gloss ceiling captures light from the terrace and gives the family room a more spacious feel. Fluted pilasters frame art and books in the Federal-style bookcase. OVERLEAF LEFT: A breakfast nook exudes comfort and character with a cork floor, tiger-maple countertops, and a custom banquette. OVERLEAF RIGHT: Bluestone pavers complement aged brick in the garden.

PRECEDING SPREAD: Art, antiques,
rare volumes all have their place,
thanks to custom millwork in the
library. OPPOSITE: The master
bedroom required only a soft
touch of new surfaces and decor.
ABOVE: A bedroom was reconfigured to accommodate present-day
needs as a study for work and a
setting for prized art and antiques.
RIGHT: In his bathroom, a wall
flanked by pilasters in honed
Botticino frames a polished nickel
sink stand with a shaped stone
top. The baseboard and floors are
Botticino with a Corinthian beige
accent border. Beyond is his dressing alcove leading to his study.

ABOVE AND OPPOSITE: By opening up the wall to the terrace and adding
French doors, the guest room is now bathed in light, and the terrace
serves as an open-air sitting room. New stucco on the parapet walls and
a floor of comfortable floating wood panels refreshed the space.

PRESERVING CHARACTER

In the countryside of the Hudson River Valley, the Doric and Ionic orders live on. From 1820 to 1850, it was considered an expression of "local nationalism and civic virtue" to build with references to ancient Greece. When our clients purchased a 120-acre farm and house dating from the 1840s, they were passionate about maintaining the historic Greek Revival character of the house. Inspired by the renovation work our firm had completed on a Greek Revival farmhouse in Kinderhook, New York, our clients asked us to preserve as much as possible of their original house, remove a 1950s addition, and establish rooms, approximately 4,800 square feet, in keeping with the Greek Revival vernacular.

This was to be our clients' country house with a fairly open, flexible program, primarily to create space for family and visiting friends. Following Greek Revival houses in the area, we added three flat-roof additions, extending the massing of the main house by more than a third. We sited and added a kitchen and breakfast room on the east side of the house, so coffee or tea might be enjoyed with the morning light. To enliven the new family room, which we imagined would be used at day's end, we sited the spot for reading, watching TV, or playing a game of chess, on the west side to capture afternoon light. A large west terrace that overlooks the pond connects the family room and guest bedroom extensions to the main house. As many of the historic windows as possible were preserved.

The dining room was the historic pearl of the house, so, in keeping with vernacular details, we salvaged flooring, trimmed the opening to the secondary stair hall with hand-hewn posts, and added exposed timber frame beams.

Thanks to the stewardship of our clients and well-considered input of interior designer Sam Blount, a simple American, as well as Greek Revival vocabulary has been preserved. Custom Shaker-inspired cabinets for the corners of the bunk room expressed simple American. Grand in their virtuosity, four fluted Doric columns on the facade have been refabricated in mahogany using the same staved fluting as the originals. There is now a solid monumentality to this country estate, a historically rich character.

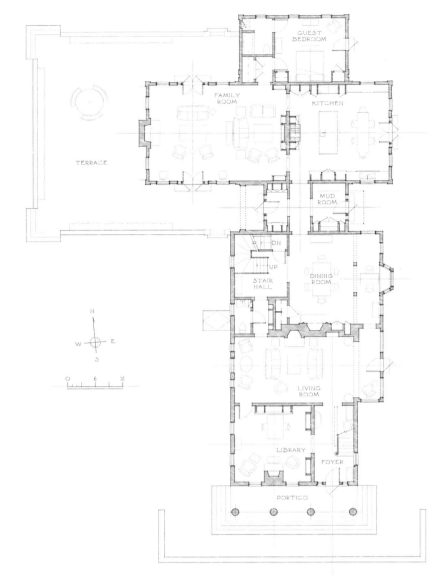

PRECEDING SPREAD: The Doric order lives on in this Greek Revival house dating from the 1840s. LEFT: Fluted columns have been refabricated in mahogany using the same staved fluting as the originals. OPPOSITE: A key element of the restoration of the main entry to the house was designing a new staircase with a graceful volute handrail and newel post terminus.

RIGHT: The dining room was the eighteenth-century original core of the house. We added character with hand-troweled plaster walls, a random-width scalloped wainscot, exposed hand-hewn posts and beams as well as antique wood plank flooring set with cut nails. The room opens to the new secondary stairs as well as the mudroom. OVERLEAF: The projecting west wing of the house is anchored with a fireplace. Fixed transoms over the double-hung windows align with the French doors and sidelights.

ABOVE: The roof material is lead-coated copper. A pent roof over the back door provides protection from the elements. OPPOSITE: The mudroom entrance has a limestone floor, beadboard wainscoting, and Greek Revival moldings. OVERLEAF: The flat roof over the kitchen wing allowed for substantially higher ceilings. Kirby stone countertops and backsplash tie to the black-painted Windsor chairs.

ABOVE: Shaker simplicity inspired the tapered newel posts and tapered square pickets of this new secondary stair. OPPOSITE: With a trayed ceiling and three exposures, this bedroom feels spacious and bright. The Shaker aesthetic is reflected in the design of a painted corner cabinet.

AN INVITING REINVENTION

Sometimes our design vision begins on one scale and, due to unexpected opportunities, joyously blossoms to another. In this case, we were initially brought in to give new life to one estate-condition apartment in a landmarked Schwartz & Gross building on Fifth Avenue. As we were developing a schematic design, the opportunity presented itself for our clients to explore a grander program when the adjacent apartment became available for purchase. Our mandate then became to design a warm and inviting full-floor residence that would balance the drama of the now sixty-five feet of Central Park and city skyline views with elegant and refined classical ornamental details, rich finishes, textures, and materials.

To create a light-filled, gracious floor plan, all existing interiors were removed so the principal rooms could be connected by enfilade along the windows overlooking Central Park. Just off the entry foyer, the new gallery now also serves as the organizing hub for the living room, library, kitchen, breakfast room, and passage to the master suite. The east wing includes a family room, which is a hub for bedrooms, music room, bar, laundry, and gym.

Once the apartment's organization was established, we then prepared a canvas for the harder finishes—millwork, plaster, patterned stone, wood moldings, and mirrors. Key living spaces are now framed by delicately pilastered thresholds. The use of eye-catching stone and plaster ornamentation in the gallery sets a rich architectural tone for the entire apartment. The generosity of space meant we could gracefully shepherd a gaze to the Central Park views by making two deep elliptical arched openings with keystones and attenuated pilasters that both entice the eye and enhance the flow for entertaining.

To lure the light from the expansive living room window through the dining room to the library and into the master bedroom, we left grand openings between these rooms but designed a custom pocketing wall that can protect the master bedroom from public view. Art installed on that wall can pass the pivoting jamb, cleverly concealing the clients' private world.

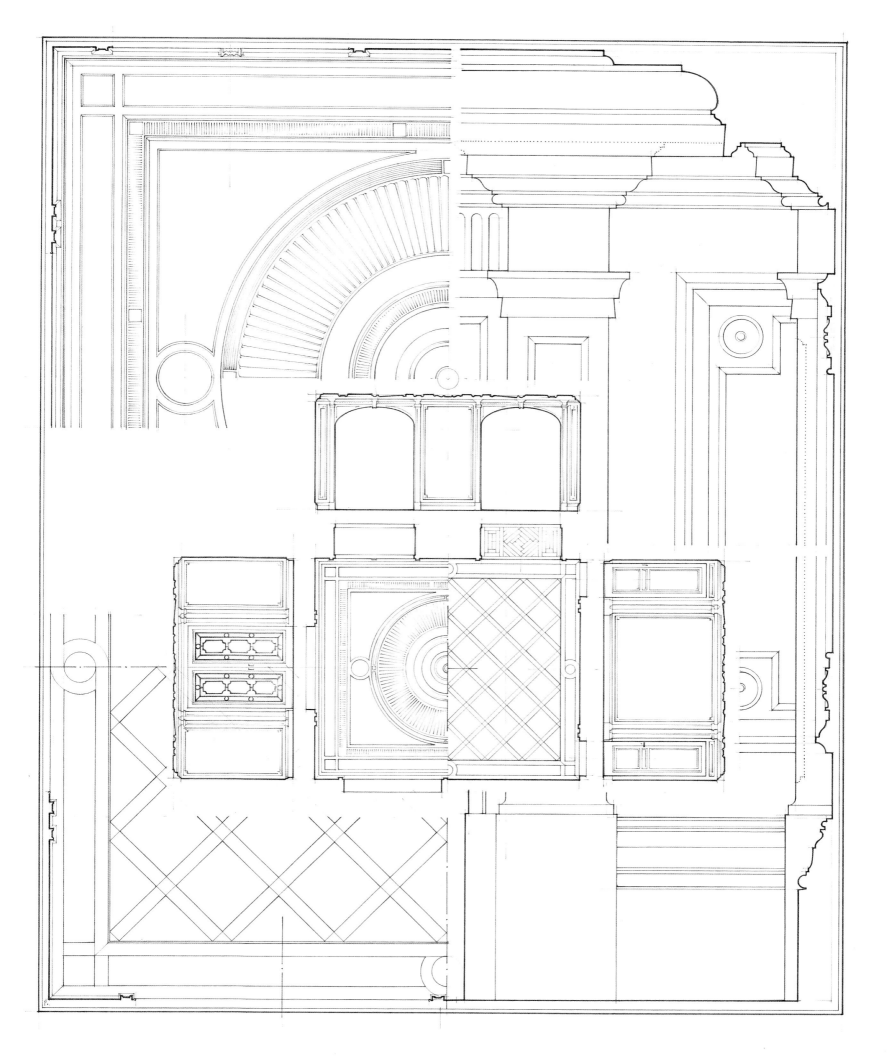

RIGHT: Two deep elliptical paneled openings with scrolled keystones and attenuated pilasters frame views of Central Park. The entrance gallery welcomes light into the interior, but it also serves as the organizing hub for the living room, library, kitchen, breakfast room, and passage to the master suite. The use of dramatic stone and plaster detailing sets a rich architectural tone for the entire apartment.

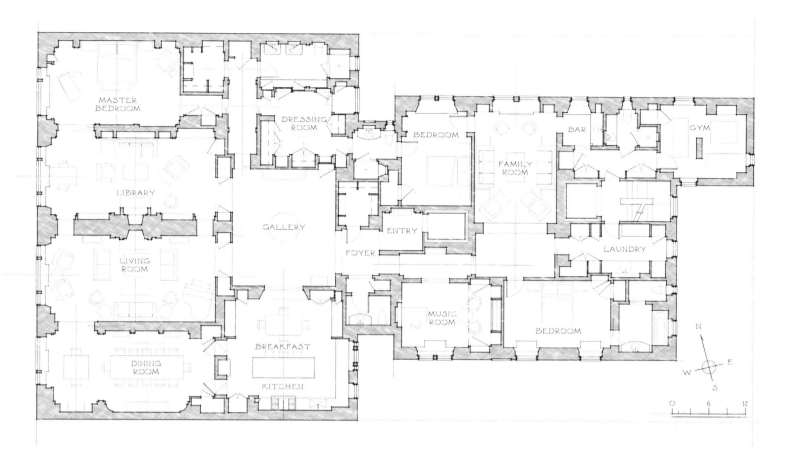

Patterned marble or white-oak floors, textured walls, embellished plaster ceilings, friezes, and moldings unite the composition, but they also provide a classical expression of distinction for each individual living space. The Laurentian and New York Public Libraries inspired the Doric architectural details of the anigré-paneled library. Art Deco references add style to the master suite. Fretwork, delicate bead-and-reel banding, and heightened cove ceilings set a dignified tone in the music room. Working in harmony with these architectural dynamics, the interior design team at Cullman & Kravis layered in softer finishes, fabrics, floor coverings, and furnishings.

Creating a space for memorably gracious entertaining was key to what our clients wished to achieve. We are so pleased that their refined vision and our teamwork with fellow designers, favored craftsmen, and artisans earned this "reinvention of a Fifth Avenue apartment" a Stanford White award.

OPPOSITE: Patterned-marble floors with inset brass banding and ornamentation, white-oak floors, textured walls, plaster moldings, and embellished cove ceilings, and French-polished mahogany doors with hand-etched art glass unite the apartment's composition. This corridor leads to the music room and the east wing of the apartment.

RIGHT: Continuing the ornamentation seen in the gallery with plaster cornice and paneled ceiling, the living room received an elegant classical articulation.

ABOVE: The dining room is designed with a paneled wood wainscot, pilasters, and a half elliptical fluted ceiling. The fan articulation on the ceiling anchors the pendant light fixtures over the dining table. OPPOSITE: To make the most of the extraordinary Central Park view, an intimate dining alcove accommodates a smaller table.

RIGHT: The French-polished anigré-paneled library frames a majestic view of Central Park. The large pocketing panel on the right leads to the master bedroom. OVERLEAF LEFT: Art Deco inspired the architectural language of the master bedroom. OVERLEAF RIGHT: The newly established principal enfilade of the apartment, from dining room to master bedroom, provides sixty-five feet of Central Park views.

ABOVE: Flanked by built-in bookcases, the guitar wall in the wood-paneled music
room conceals a fold-down bed. OPPOSITE: Delicate bead-and-reel banding
and circular coved roundels embellish the corners of the music room ceiling.

Curating for a New Season

Changes in life's seasons can call for a change of view, a change of space and how it is configured. In this case, our client was making the leap from the West Side of Manhattan to the East Side, changing a view, changing space and its arrangement. Our clients' challenge to us: from all angles make the most of a fresh view of Central Park. Our firm had already completed three other projects in this 1927 J. E. R. Carpenter-designed building, so we were very familiar with the infrastructure and how to work efficiently with the building's schedule.

The interior space of this apartment is a little over 2,000 square feet. We reconfigured the exterior wall to add three custom steel French doors leading out to the expansive terrace, gaining a grand outdoor space for breakfasts and suppers al fresco. The glass doors let light and air into the apartment and, thanks to the customized feature of a smaller window within a door, are able to capture a cool breeze even with the doors closed. The addition of a retractable awning means the extra "room" is also available on the brightest of days.

For this new season of life our clients refined their collection to accommodate streamlined single-floor living. Working with the singularly adroit "curators" at Cullman & Kravis, we conceived spaces to honor Picasso, Matisse, Cassatt, Pissarro, Archipenko, Botero. To honor the art of Central Park, we replaced all windows; that refresh gives the sense of looking out from a precious cabinet. Every detail was thoughtfully considered to make the very most of available space and appeal to the refined aesthetic of our clients. An English custom-carved white marble mantel with a limestone surround and hearth was added to give the living room a focal point and provide an ideal space for the Picasso. Architectural ornaments salvaged from the owners' past were integrated into the new outdoor space.

In the dining room an antiqued and beveled mirrored door with bespoke unlacquered brass hardware disguises a very specifically designed mini-office for her in a room with a dramatic view. All nooks and crannies were also put to use in the master bedroom, where closets, hidden from view, provide a depth of storage. Custom cabinetry in the living room frames a cherished book collection and features brass pulls that extend small shelves for resting a book or even a guest's drink.

New seasons and changes in life are inevitable. In this particular space, the process of addressing new needs and articulating space to accommodate for those needs was sheer joy. At project's end our work together was described as "perfection." Park perfection.

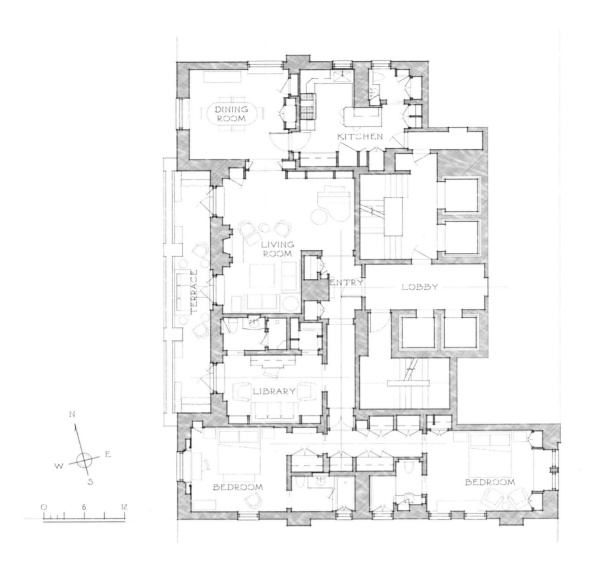

LEFT: This passage extends past the library entrance to the right and connects to a master dressing hall with Harmon doors neatly concealed. The two-toned, diagonally patterned oak floors work well as the hall direction turns. RIGHT: Antiqued mirrored glass with églomisé banding and corner motifs enriches this entry hall composition.

RIGHT: To bring the maximum amount of light into the living room, we added tall transomed French doors with integral window ventilation panels. The reflective high-gloss ceiling adds a further dimension. OVERLEAF LEFT: New double-hung windows in the dining room make the most of the Central Park view. OVERLEAF RIGHT: A retractable awning protects the terrace on the brightest days.

RIGHT: Below a woven, banded ornamental plaster ceiling, the library's custom millwork in French-polished anigré includes a pull-out shelf and an integrated desk.

ABOVE: Her bath is a serene space, with a coved plaster ceiling, white marble paneled walls, and Bleu de Savoie wainscot banding, countertop, tub deck, and floor borders. OPPOSITE: A view through the dressing hall to the master bedroom. Translucent mirror panels on the corridor closets expand the narrow space.

A Barn of Dreams

Architects like to imagine themselves as structural and aesthetic "dream-catchers." It may sound romantic, but, at our best, we "catch" clients' dreams and bring them to life. We recently tested this whimsical "build a dream and they will come" philosophy on Mason Hill Farm in Columbia County, some 130 miles north of New York City. Our clients had previously asked us to restore the Greek Revival farmhouse on the property. More than a decade later, we were asked to return to consider the stone remnants of a barn foundation tucked into a dramatic bank of earth as an inspiration for a twenty-first-century barn that would make sense within the context of the land and its history.

We worked with the barn preservationists at the New Jersey Barn Company to rescue a 1780s barn, originally found standing in Locktown, New Jersey. The owners of Mason Hill Farm had purchased the historic white-oak hand-hewn bank barn and were brainstorming its twenty-first-century purpose. Our clients wished to create a grand space appealing to its musicians, film aficionados, readers, writers, and yogis.

With the owners, we drew inspiration from visits to Monticello, Hancock Shaker Village, and the New England craftsmen still making period iron and woodwork historically in keeping with the eighteenth-century vernacular of the frame. As we began working, it became clear that the family wanted a peaceful, sun-strewn space, a barn that could house a celebration, a hootenanny, a film screening, the car, the tractor, even a Steinway piano—or two. Since the family had grown, they needed space for a holiday table that could host more and more family and friends.

At Monticello we were mesmerized by Thomas Jefferson's weather vane. Mounted on the roof and connected to a compass rose on the ceiling of the east portico, the weather vane tells the wind direction both inside and out. For months, we looked skyward at every turn. Weather vanes, spinning icons, banners. Sketches on napkins were blown up into full-scale renderings and tracing-paper patterns for a Virginia blacksmith to fashion into a six-foot-wide stainless-steel wind-inspired pennant.

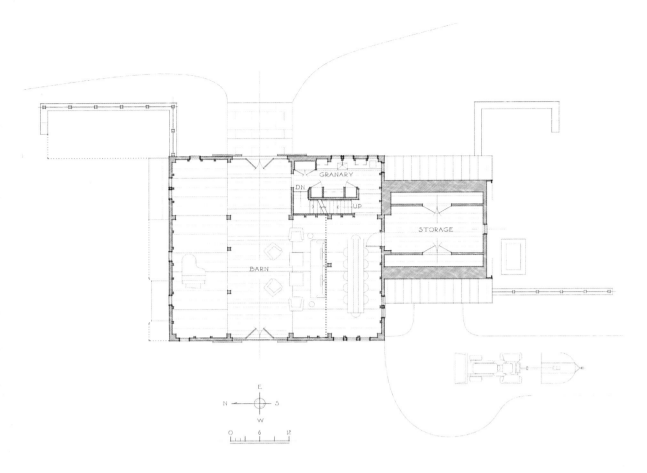

PRECEDING SPREAD: The white barn connects to the Greek Revival farmhouse to the north. BELOW: Exposed zinc bands inserted every sixth course of cedar shingles will preserve the roofing material. Sitting naturally on the sloping grade, the barn gives the impression that it has always been there. OPPOSITE: The foundation walls are local bed-set fieldstone.

GRANARY

DN

UP

STORAGE

BARN

N E S W

0 6 12

The round barn at Hancock Shaker Village influenced the decision to recreate a "dairy" on the cooler lower floor of the barn by whitewashing the original bark-covered timber beams and handcrafted plaster walls. Essex green was selected for the screen-storm doors set just behind the barn's sliding doors to effectively make these doors nearly invisible from the exterior when the white sliding doors are open.

The original granary of the barn translated into a state-of-the-art kitchen featuring countertops cut of Church Hill Reserve soapstone from the Alberene Quarry in Virginia, the only remaining domestically quarried soapstone. An authentic oak and hemlock threshing floor was salvaged from a nineteenth-century Pennsylvania barn. A custom-designed galvanized hog-wire balustrade framed with rough-sawn white oak helped to transform the hayloft into an occasional sleeping loft, its flooring preserved from the original barn.

The late eighteenth-century hand-hewn frame with chiseled Roman numeral marriage marks uses gunstock posts in each bent, an English framing technique dating to medieval times. But this is not a drafty medieval barn. Insulation is concealed between the interior skin of shiplap boards and exterior clapboard. Outswing awning windows feature energy-efficient insulated glass. All operable windows have inswing casement sashes with invisible screens. Linear LED lights, concealed above each of the five tie beams, illuminate the white-oak rafters and band-sawn hemlock ceiling boards.

Repeatedly we returned to Shaker simplicity and functionality for inspiration. The owners' appreciation of early American history married with modern minimalist comfort now serves the family's evolving needs. The bank barn stands firm in the landscape as if a living reminder of the farm's original inhabitants, yet today the Mason Hill Farm family has dreamed up a barn where the smells are of baking croissants or Thanksgiving turkey, the sounds are of cello and piano strains, the views are of cinematic action or snowy or green pastures. This barn is a vibrant space for creativity and contemplation.

OPPOSITE: The barn now stands where the original barn had long since returned to the earth.
OVERLEAF: The threshing floor was salvaged from a nineteenth-century Pennsylvania barn. Present meets the past with the installation of radiant heating beneath all reclaimed barn flooring.

PRECEDING SPREAD LEFT: The "granary" kitchen features custom-fabricated cabinets in rustic white oak. A Church Hill Reserve soapstone countertop and backsplash surround the farmhouse porcelain sink. PREVIOUS SPREAD, CLOCKWISE FROM LEFT: A directional arrow on the compass rose of the cupola indicates the wind direction; the bents, studs, girts, wind brace, and rafters are rough-hewn white oak, c. 1780; Roman numeral marriage marks are chiseled in every assembly point of the original bents. OPPOSITE: The dining table, modeled after a nineteenth-century oak Shaker trestle table, accommodates fourteen black Windsor chairs. ABOVE: The timber structure and ceiling boards of the dairy are whitewashed with milk paint, a finish commonly found in dairy barns.

HONORING THE HEIGHT

Space, light, movement. When ceilings soar to eleven feet, the feeling of grandeur and gracious serenity is inevitable. Here the challenge was to take the approximately 2,700 square feet of Park Avenue apartment to its bare bones and reconsider the space anew. Our clients' evolving art collection was a constant source of inspiration: how and where best to view the Vik Muniz, to contemplate the John Chamberlain.

This building, designed in 1916 by J. E. R. Carpenter, acknowledged as the "father of the modern large apartment in New York," had seen various configurations, but the original footprint is still evident here. We changed the floor plan to allow a more tailored entry gallery to flow into the dining room. Cream marble flooring visually connects the gallery and dining room in one long procession. To better appreciate paintings and sculpture from various perspectives, these spatial long-view moments became a repeated theme. Find the axes, maintain the depth of space, arrange rooms so they appear to blend from one to the other, always creating views. What is that wonderful work here? There, beyond? The view from the entry gallery travels through the dining room and ends with a painting in the bedroom hall.

Honoring the extraordinary height of the rooms was another repeated program inspiration. We were invited to depart from the established cannon and invent plaster ceiling details that draw the eye up but startle in their form. The fun came in presenting our imaginative clients with different versions of a cornice detail and, in our back and forth, ending with a wide scalloped ceiling profile that looks timeless, contemporary and, most importantly, speaks to their particular aesthetic. Another strategy to keep the space open and complement the height of the rooms was the choice to custom-fabricate tall, elegant doors. The signature door of the residence is a three-paneled design featuring a reeded match-strike articulation in the middle panel.

When we excavated the space that would become the dining room, a blocked-up window was uncovered. An occasion for light, which, with our Beaux-Arts proclivities, we never pass up! At our clients' behest, we collaborated with interior designer David Kleinberg to add a jewel to the residence, a bar that provides the perfect backdrop to the view from the dining room. With honed black travertine counters, lacquer-finished cabinets with doors and shelves of Starfire glass, and polished nickel hardware, the bar literally sparkles. Pocket doors of deep-etched Silk glass, between the bar and the kitchen, are open or

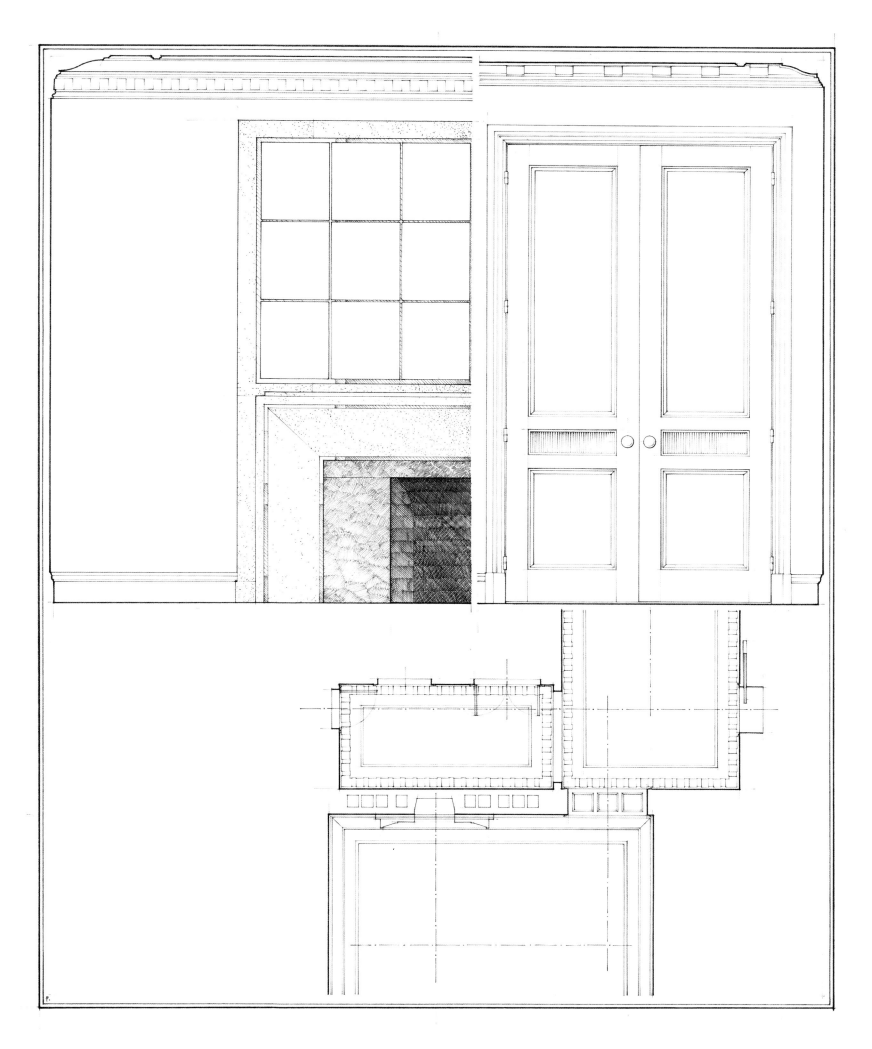

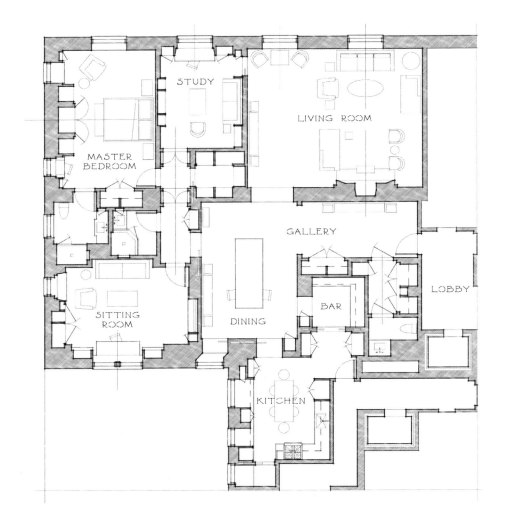

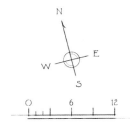

closed depending on the need for discretion. Since the bar now seems such a striking extension of the dining room, no door was necessary, but to separate the dining room from the kitchen, we designed a pocket door with translucent glass that is a symmetrical twin to one that provides light from the newly discovered window.

Light and space inspired our custom design of the honed limestone chimney breast and mantel that anchor the living room. Polished nickel banding in the mantel lends a unique artistic note. For depth and contrast, the firebox and surround are of honed black slate. Over the hearth two nine-paneled mirrors capture outdoor light and visually open the space. With the drama of a theater stage, two "curtains" of mirror slide apart to reveal a source of entertainment, a large flat-screen monitor. The chimney breast was deliberately designed to not touch the cornice line, the better to conceal its hidden agenda and balance with the deep monumental doorway leading to the dining room on its right.

Kitchens are an important space of functional innovation for us. In this apartment, we were asked to transform a tiny kitchen, staff bedroom, and bathroom into a more open setting serving a variety of

needs. We created a laundry area, stripped back any fussy aesthetic and made a light, airy room with white-oak plank floors, honed Calacatta marble countertops, and reserved-in-its-simplicity cabinetry to provide generous custom-designed storage space. In the study, the custom-created cerused oak cabinetry with state-of-the-art shelf lighting now showcases the client's antique radio-and-clock collections.

Works of art, bold and ethereal, informed a program for living that majestically frames colorful and textural expression in many different forms in a way that is as highly refined as it is functional.

ABOVE AND OPPOSITE: Views from the dining room to the gallery and to the living room.
OVERLEAF: To attract light, the cornice is composed of angled planes. Light also inspired the design of the honed limestone chimney breast and mantel. Over the hearth two nine-paneled mirrors capture outdoor light and visually open the space. The two "curtains" of mirror slide apart to reveal the source of entertainment, a flat-screen monitor.

ABOVE: The height of each room was emphasized to create walls for showcasing art.
OPPOSITE: Simple millwork in the sitting room provides display space for works of art
and amplifies the view and the light. The signature door of the residence is a
three-paneled design featuring a reeded match strike articulation in the middle panel.

ABOVE: We uncovered a blocked window, and since the light was more welcome than the view, we installed a pocket screen door that matches the door to the kitchen. The dining room is now a room of connections—to the kitchen, to the bar, to the living room, to the entry. OPPOSITE: A tiny bedroom and bath became an open kitchen with Calacatta marble counters and backsplash.

PRECEDING SPREAD: The master bedroom features an inventive plaster cornice and a reeded match-strike motif in the custom cabinets. ABOVE: Her bathroom is Bianco Dolomiti marble with mirrors framed in polished nickel. OPPOSITE: A doorway connecting the cerused oak study to the living room adds a sense of flow and light.

REFINED DETAIL

The bones were good, but in estate condition, and the composition did not make sense for a family with two children. Here we were presented with approximately 3,500 square feet in a Neo-Renaissance style building by Schwartz & Gross on Central Park West. Our clients asked for a new floor plan tailored to the family's specific needs.

Their aesthetic is serene, nuanced, so all detail, finishes, and materials mattered. Through a tall double-wide pocket door the dining room opens up from the gallery. In the dining room, we articulated the walls with flat lacquered panels and antique mirror doors, one of which serves as a discreet entry to the kitchen. The square plan of the room allows for a raised circular ceiling panel.

We took the five existing structural beams of the living room and added two crossbeams concealing integrated art lighting to create a high-gloss coffered ceiling that dramatizes the height of the room.

By removing a large corner bedroom, with interior designer Donald MacDonald, we were able to create a family room with built-in shelves for books and curios and a wall of mirror to attract natural light and play with the feeling of space. Tall three-panel French-polished crotched-mahogany sliding doors add distinction between the family room and bar and the living room and the bar. The warmth of mahogany was also used in the bar, a dry bar, that serves both the family room and the living room.

The floorplan was reconfigured so that the two children's bedrooms and the master bedroom are all off the same hall and each child has an en-suite bathroom. Not surprisingly, we were asked to establish a spacious eat-in kitchen. In order to achieve this, we modified the dining room to capture space for a built-in banquette that easily seats six.

It was, however, in the entry gallery where our clients truly made their artistic statement. Airy, indirectly lit from above and within, it is from the gallery that the movement of the apartment radiates. We designed a rich, deep opening between the gallery and the living room for illuminated display cabinets in both the gallery and the living room to showcase a colorful porcelain collection. The gallery cornice was kept low to engage with pilasters framing the door to the living room and the display niches. Coved lighting anchors the internal space of the gallery to give it an exemplary level of refinement and pronounce the entrance into a family space of graceful tranquility.

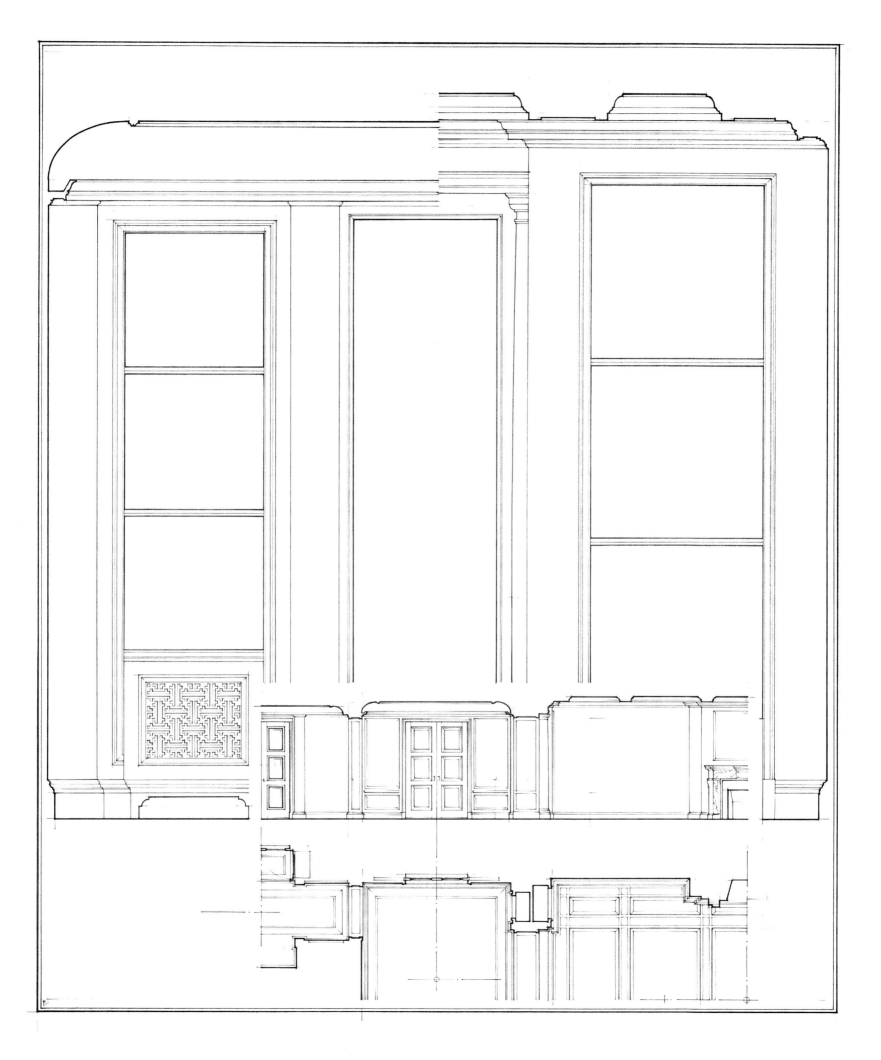

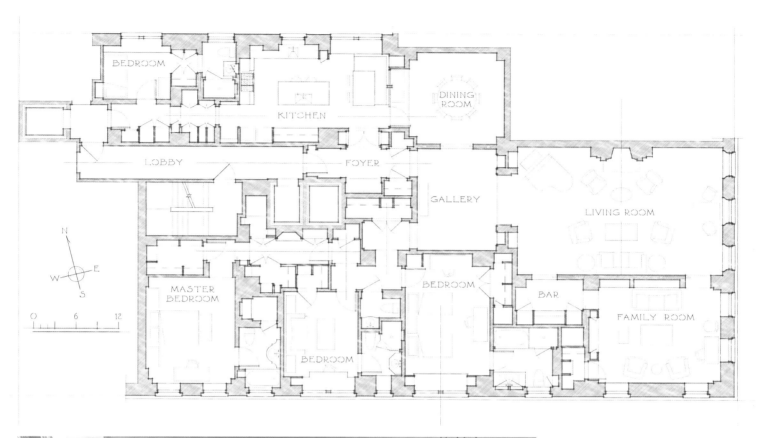

OPPOSITE: A small foyer, with dark gray walls and a coved ceiling, leads to the generous gallery. LEFT: We designed a rich, deep opening between the gallery and the living room where illuminated cabinets display the porcelain collection. The cornice engages the pilasters framing the doorway and the niches to create a serene and unified composition.

PRECEDING SPREAD: In the living room, we added two crossbeams concealing integrated art lighting to create a flat-paneled plaster coffered ceiling that dramatizes the height of the room. OPPOSITE: With the mahogany pocket door open, there is an ease of movement from the living room to the family room. ABOVE: A wall of antiqued mirror adds an expansive character to the family room.

ABOVE LEFT: Fragile blossoms on silver leaf, a Greek key frieze, a black lacquered vanity with nickel legs standing on a mix of dark and light Emperador marble: a powder room of refined detail. ABOVE RIGHT: The bar is figured mahogany with an églomisé-banded antiqued mirror backsplash and black and gold marble countertop with polished nickel hardware. OPPOSITE: Sheathed in blue lacquer, the dining room has antiqued mirror doors, one of which serves as a discreet entry to the kitchen.

RIGHT: With a slight build-out of the left and right corners of the room, we concealed the beam to create a bed alcove trimmed with a beaded plaster return.

ABOVE: The master dressing room features an oak herringbone floor and an integrated dresser with a shaped-edge statuary marble countertop and a three-way mirror. OPPOSITE: Centering the vanity on the entry door of the master bathroom is key to this spacious composition. Other graceful touches: a bow-fronted vanity, Calacatta Gold marble on a Calacatta mosaic field.

CREATING CONNECTIONS

Back to the city, back to a time when design and living considerations no longer needed to revolve around the children. Having raised their children, our clients could now conceive of an urban footprint where they could showcase their art and Americana collection, relax with a book, destress with a sweaty workout, even "host" the children in a more grown-up context.

We began with a full floor, about 4,000 square feet, of a 1930 building designed with some Art Deco flourishes by Van Wart & Wein. And we began an extraordinary design relationship of mutual admiration.

Our clients' charge to us was to give the apartment a classical articulation that would serve as a dignified backdrop for their collection of museum-quality furniture and artwork. First impressions set the tone, so we savored the process of designing a memorable entry door and sidelights of handmade restoration glass that permits natural light to bathe the intimate foyer, but is also secure. A metalwork artisan specially crafted the planished ornamental details in patinated bronze and wrought iron. The floral medallion in the plaster overdoor effortlessly engages with the organic metalwork detail of the door. The tone of quiet sophistication has been set.

Blessed with a living room enjoying south and west exposures, we created connections where there were none. Using discreet hinged and pocket doors, we connected the living room to the dining room and to the library, effectively drawing natural light into the living room from four directions—its own windows as well as those of the dining room and library.

We reoriented the library to face west so that the room enjoys lateral light from the living room as well as from its own windows to the south. French-polished and figured anigré custom-fabricated millwork made the library an important book room with a concealed television.

Details in the dining room also exhibit an appreciation of classical detail as an architectural frame. Working with a small alcove, we added an ornamental plaster cornice and elliptical plaster ceiling bands to define the dining room. These architectural nuances provocatively balance the bold yellows and blues of contemporary paintings. Architecture and art are in creative conversation and connect past and present.

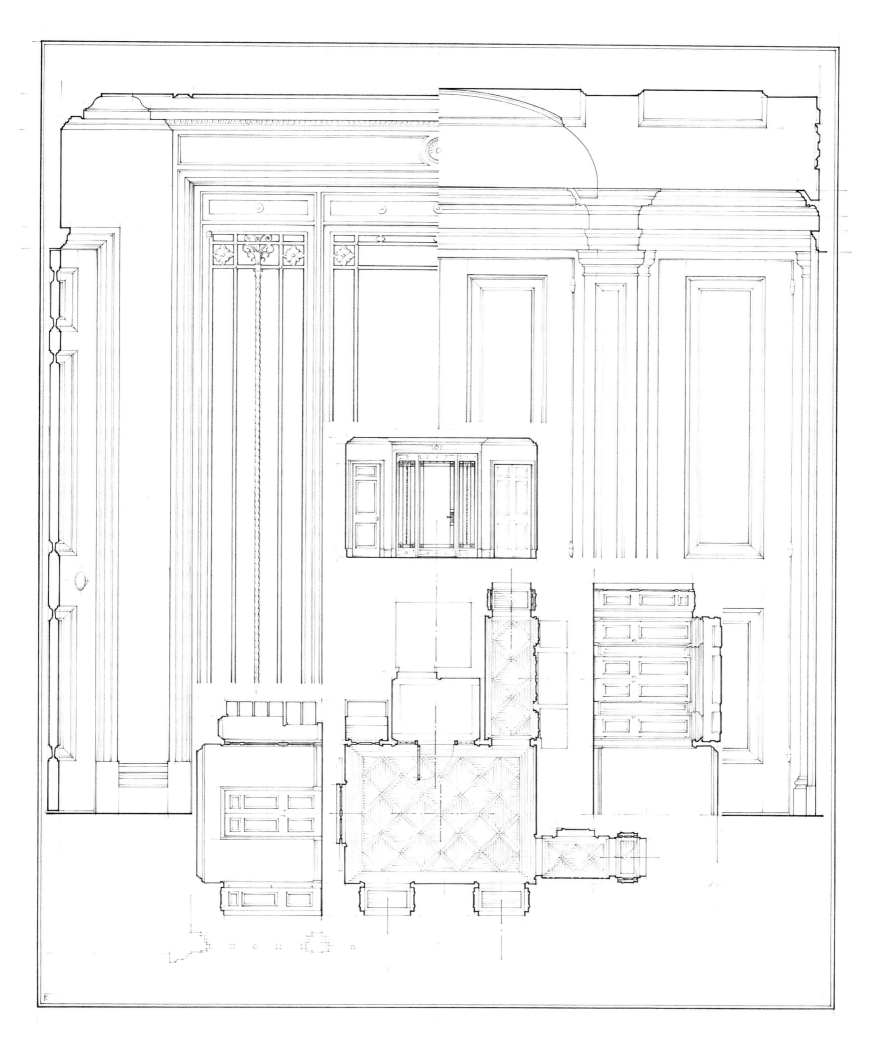

OPPOSITE: The entry door is artisan-crafted in bronze and wrought iron. The egg-and-dart and central floral medallion of the overdoor cornice engages with the organic detail of the door. RIGHT AND FAR RIGHT: The trabeated hall with French-polished mahogany doors has a paneled vaulted ceiling above a plaster cornice.

RIGHT: The living room enjoys southern and western exposures. City views are better appreciated through inswing casement windows with a fixed transom. Each window opening is framed in a paneled millwork concealing dual blackout and solar motorized shades as well as a radiator enclosure with honed crema marfil marble tops.

ABOVE: Harmon hinged pocket doors connect the living room to the library, the entry gallery, and the dining room, admitting natural light to the interior of the apartment. OPPOSITE: Beneath an ornate plaster mantel, dark Emperador marble frames the soapstone inner fireplace surround.

PRECEDING SPREAD LEFT: Elliptical plaster ceiling details and an ornate cornice were added to architecturally define the dining room and its alcove. PRECEDING SPREAD RIGHT: Painted-wood panels, bracket-supported upper cabinets, burnished nickel hardware, and oak planked floors give the kitchen a timeless character. RIGHT: French-polished, figured anigré millwork below a coved plaster ceiling makes the library a distinguished room.

RIGHT: In the master bedroom, a classical articulation in the cornice and plaster mantel creates a dignified setting for important paintings and American folk art.

ABOVE LEFT: His dressing room is handsomely paneled in French-polished anigré. ABOVE RIGHT:
Custom-fabricated elliptical mirrors are suspended over basins set in a painted wood and
honey onyx vanity with antiqued-gold-plated hardware and fittings. OPPOSITE: A pendentive
vaulted ceiling in her bathroom rises above walls of tinted plaster, white marble, and onyx.
The pewter bow-fronted washstand with ormolu decoration continues the classical theme.

A Place in Nature

When we are able to continue the creative process with a client, we truly understand the maxim "architecture lives." In 2004 we restored a farm property in southern New England, which included an eighteenth-century Federal main house, as well as a nineteenth-century cottage and two new barn structures with antique timber frames. Eight years later, we were invited to return to the rural setting to site a swimming pool, pool house, and pergola. The program included a kitchen, outdoor barbecue grill, pergola, changing room, powder room, outdoor shower, and mechanical storage room. The timeless simplicity of the pool and pool house composition refer to the farm's early American roots and earned a Stanford White award as a sympathetic addition to the property.

A critical component was the siting of the pool and pool house on a slope that included a restored half-acre pond with a traditional weir. The design intent was to take advantage of the changing grade by building a terraced area for the pool, which naturally created a ha-ha wall enclosing part of the recreational area. The ha-ha wall makes a vertical barrier without interrupting the view of the pond and landscape beyond. The remainder of the pool area was enclosed with a fence inspired by the paddock fencing on the property.

The pool was designed to honor the land. With landscape architect Eric Groft of Oehme, Van Sweden & Associates, we designed a pool with coping that is slightly submerged, allowing the water to continuously overflow the perimeter. This unique edge detail creates the illusion that the pool is a pond. Plantings undulate close to the edge, complementing the overall design.

The design of the pool house was informed by the architecture of the farm buildings—the sliding barn doors, the stonework of the barbecue chimney, the exterior beadboard cladding with expressed pegs, and the hand-split cedar roof shakes. Barn-like doors with restoration glass panes open to reveal a

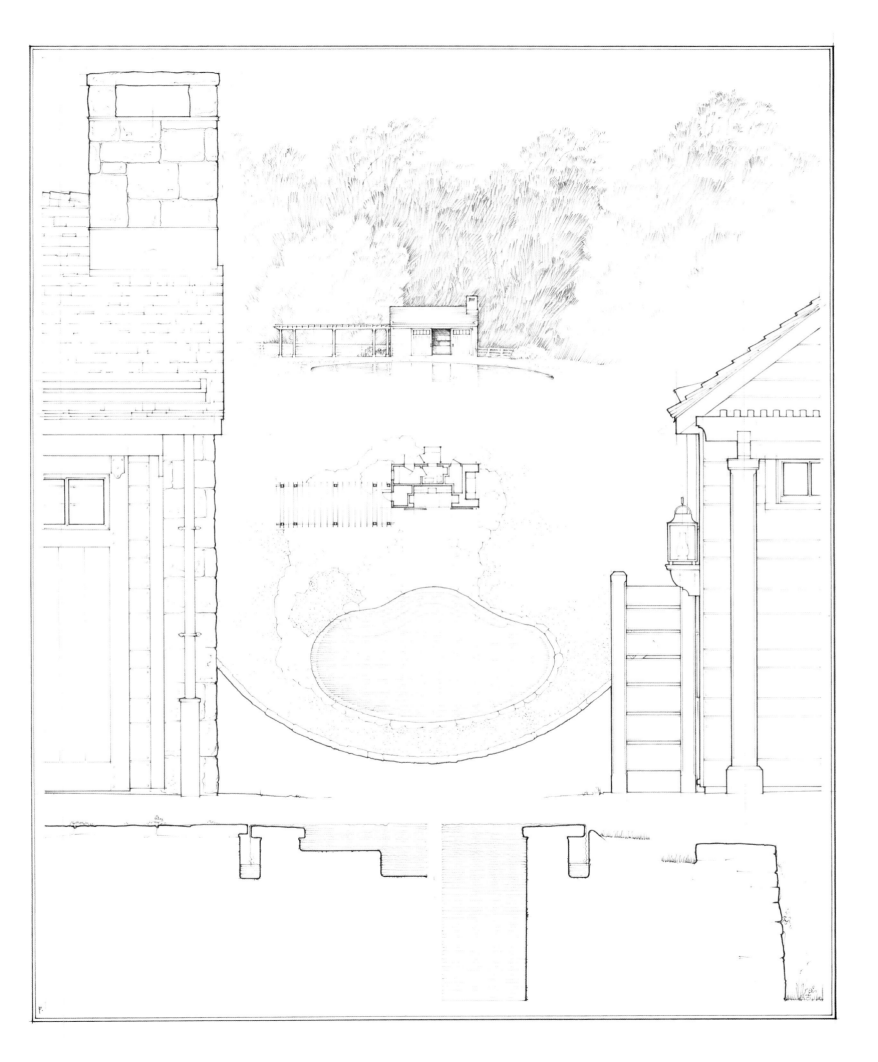

LEFT: The design intent was to create a simple gabled structure with a stone chimney reminiscent of a historic farm outbuilding. The paddock-style gate and fence transition into a ha-ha wall that encompasses the naturalistic pool and view to the restored pond.

kitchen alcove anchored with a central farmhouse sink. The kitchen is fitted with oil-rubbed teak cabinetry and a Kirby stone countertop. The changing room and powder room are accessed from the rear, where there is also an outdoor shower.

The north end is anchored by a chimney of local fieldstone laid in a manner similar to the stone foundations of the main house. A teak pergola extends to the south. The traditional details include painted posts with coved corners and beaded caps set on Roxbury granite plinths. Painted beams with shaped tails support teak purlins and slats left natural to age over time. The closely positioned slats provide a shaded area without the need for greenery coverage. The posts, beams, and purlins are all capped with lead-coated copper flashing to protect the wood.

Architecture for soaking in the ever-changing wonders of the great outdoors.

OPPOSITE: Pool water slips over a slightly canted Roxbury granite coping into a narrow slot that runs the entire perimeter of the pool's edge. ABOVE: The front facade includes a pair of barn-like doors, which slide open to reveal a kitchen alcove with a central farmhouse sink.

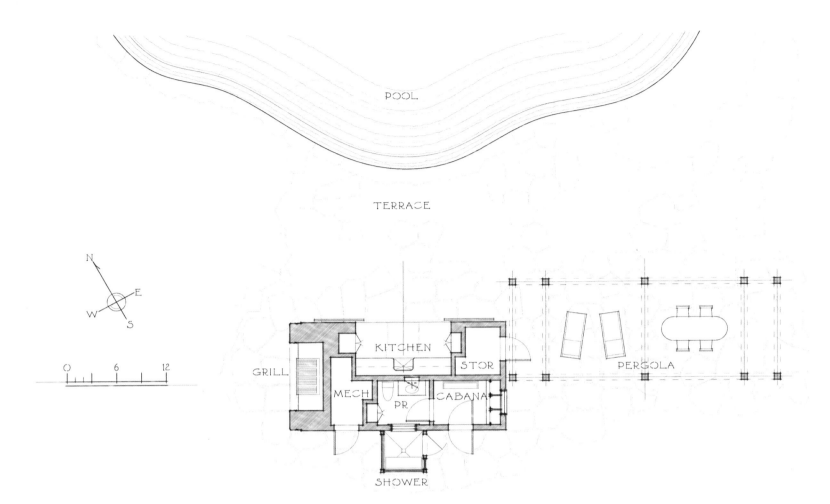

POOL

TERRACE

N
E
W
S

0   6   12

GRILL

KITCHEN

STOR

MECH

PR

CABANA

PERGOLA

SHOWER

FAR LEFT: The architectural simplicity of horizontal, random-width beadboard with pegged joinery references the early American roots of the farm. LEFT: The outdoor shower is enclosed with teak posts and beaded fence boards. OPPOSITE: Landscaping beds with indigenous plantings close to the pool's edge complement pool and site design.

ABOVE: A teak pergola over a Roxbury granite terrace creates a shaded refuge for lounging and dining. Underground irrigation supports the growth of green moss between the granite pavers. OPPOSITE: Barbecue equipment is set within a hearth-like alcove lined in granite blocks. OVERLEAF: Sited beyond the horse paddocks above the ha-ha wall, the pool house overlooks the restored pond.

TO SERVE THE MANY

Houses can serve many purposes. In this instance, the house in question, originally built in 1871 as a private home, has been the residence of more than one university president. Now the building receives visiting dignitaries, world leaders, and university patrons and offers a welcoming setting for greeting freshmen, bidding seniors farewell, and hosting university friends and family.

The original architect was Russell Sturgis Jr., but more than a century later, when we were asked to work with local lead architects Charney Architects, much of the original Victorian Gothic style turrets and gables had been modified to present a restrained Georgian Revival house more in keeping with the other brick buildings of this New England university. Our role in this renovation was to bring our classical aesthetic to guide exterior and landscape concepts, to oversee a comprehensive interior renovation, and to collaborate with the university as well as with interior designer Thomas Jayne of Jayne Design Studio.

Before we could set the program, we interviewed many of the people who regularly work in the house to find out demands on the spaces, their purpose, size, and functional requirements. We updated the 20,570-square-foot building's electrical, mechanical, plumbing, fire protection, lighting, and A/V systems and set in place this century's latest technology and ecofriendly materials in a way that seamlessly fit with the building's historic fabric. Specifically, we installed minimum water usage plumbing fittings and extremely efficient air-conditioning and replaced window glass with insulated glazing to eliminate the need for storm windows.

The process took us back to our academic days and the rigor of the Beaux-Arts ideal. An unexpected opportunity to bring in Beaux-Arts thinking presented itself when we visited and spoke with the

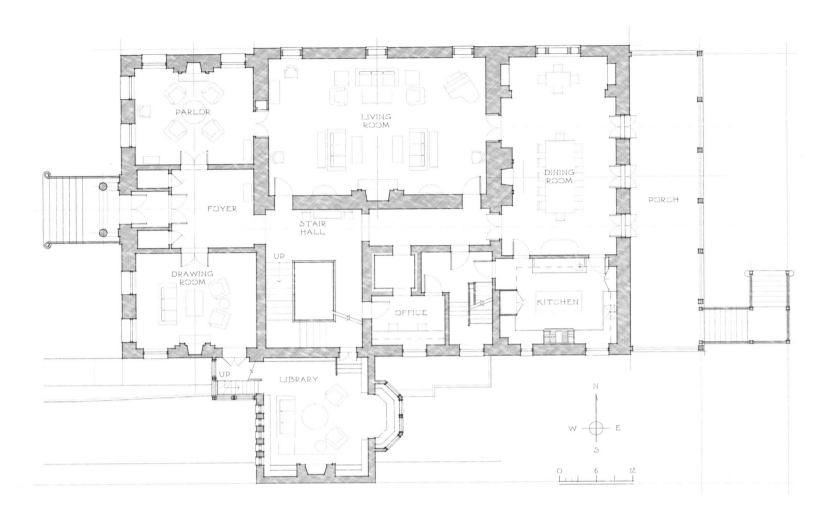

university president's staff whose workspace was on the lower level of the house. With our commitment to capturing natural light for interior space, we realized that if we lowered and enlarged windows and reconfigured the offices, storeroom, and small staff kitchen, we could create a corridor to the light that would enliven the office areas.

With a full calendar of entertaining and events in the house, the project focused on putting in place state-of-the-art catering kitchens, reconsidering flow to address staff and chef requests for enhanced functionality, and improving public bathrooms.

The major public rooms display paintings, both nineteenth-century and contemporary master-works, from the university's collection. Our restoration work included the installation of air-conditioning

OPPOSITE: Honoring the history of this Georgian Revival house, updating, refreshing, and bringing windows, entrances and exits up to code was our mandate. New windows with more energy-efficient insulated glazing eliminate the need for storm windows.

and heating systems in keeping with current art conservation standards.

At times, it felt as if we were discovering hidden gems of the house's history. In one intimate historic room, we were able to bring a semi-forgotten fireplace back to working condition. When we removed built-in bookshelves to open spaces for more practical use, we uncovered more original history: two stained-glass windows.

Those multifaceted and hued windows are, perhaps, an icon for the many purposes and people this historic house has served and now will ever elegantly and ably continue to serve.

ABOVE AND OPPOSITE: As the architects orchestrating interiors, we guided the installation of new concelaed art lighting for both public and private spaces and new sconce and pendant lighting to enhance the existing staircase.

RIGHT: The house not only hosts visiting dignitaries but also serves as a gallery for paintings and objects from the university's collection. We consulted on appropriate lighting for both living and display. OVERLEAF LEFT AND RIGHT: An important element of working with an existing structure is knowing what to touch, what not to touch. Here we restored the existing cornice and door entablature and installed state-of-the-art lighting.

PRECEDING SPREAD: A simple cornice at the high ceiling and a chair rail create a generous wall that accommodates both historic portraits and dramatic abstract art. ABOVE: With new doors leading to the porch, air-conditioning, lighting, and damask wallpaper, the dining room is an inviting, comfortable space for entertaining faculty, students, and visiting speakers. OPPOSITE: The custom-designed mantel is in keeping with historic precedents.

PRECEDING SPREAD: New French doors and transoms in the dining room
open to the porch. OPPOSITE: To harness exterior light from the rear garden,
lower level offices have been reconfigured and two pairs of French doors
installed. ABOVE: Within the canopy of trees is the private living space.

ACKNOWLEDGMENTS

First and foremost, I would like to express my deep gratitude to my clients. Nothing pleases me more than to hear from you how our designed living spaces have brought joy and ease to your day-to-day, or to be invited back to transform your homes for a new phase of life.

I am truly indebted to my talented staff: associates Tim Middleton, Adam Platt, John Pelligra; project architects Christine Song, Matthew Wanner, Andrea Wang, Tomer Tal, Erin de Losier, Izumi Shepard, William Clarke, José Quezada, Julia Fishman, Jennifer Lee, Bisma Sarfaraz, and Grimaldi Perdomo. And my support staff: managing director Elizabeth Heilman Brooke Murray, business manager Moses Uriu, assistants Suzanne Walker, Monica Mulvany, and Janeth Diaz. Specific thanks to José Quezada for his steadfast work preparing all floor plans. I'd like to also recognize former employees for their valuable contributions: design associate Charlotte Worthy, marketing director Triveni Masopust, and project architect Joel Pidel.

The softer finishes of our projects, provided by interior designers, play a crucial part in the success of our work. In each chapter I have made a point to recognize the many talents shown here. I would particularly like to thank Ellie Cullman and her team at C & K for more than two decades of rewarding collaborations.

Thanks to consultants CBBLD, CES, Bob Divilio, Bill Drakeley, Jim MacDonald, Greg Saum, Jacquie Mosca, and Nat Oppenheimer of Silman. Thanks to Paul Austi for bringing twenty-first-century technology to many of our projects. Thanks to artisans Robert Baird and Steve Brown, Elric J. Endersby and Alexander Greenwood, Gaston & Wyatt, Fred Martin, Robert Meehan Jr., Dan Rundell, and Adrian Taylor.

I never underestimate the importance of teaming up with builders who can orchestrate the precision and quality of our designs. Accordingly, I would like to thank the contractors whose work is shown in this book: Michael Vella, Kenneth Bacco, Dimeo Construction, Vincent DiSalvo, Steve Fetner, Peter Hammer, IMI, George Kral, Pete Mostaccio, Steven Moy, Guido D. Rebosio Jr., Thomas Rogan, Thomas Stephens, and Nick Stern. Thank you, Peter Cosola, for more than twenty years of gratifying teamwork.

I also would like to recognize the contributions of landscape designers Renée Byers, Wendy P. Carroll, Eric Groft, and Drew Zambelli

Seeing the detail, the color, the character of our work is what this book is all about. It has been an exciting visual journey with talented photographers: Bruce Buck, Pieter Estersohn, Nick Johnson, Francesco Lagnese, Scott Langley, Eric Roth, Durston Saylor, Simon Upton, and Bjorn Wallander and stylists Howard Christian and Anita Sarsidi.

Many thanks for the enthusiastic support of the Institute of Classical Architecture and Art.

Thank you, Tom Maciag. for creating the firm's website and keeping us ahead of the curve with media outreach.

I am sincerely appreciative of Jill Cohen's expertise and guidance in establishing my relationship with the Monacelli Press and for introducing me to Elizabeth White. Elizabeth's mindful skill with the text and images here and her organized calm have made the business of publishing a pleasure. Book designers Doug Turshen and Steve Turner, please know your patience and considered care in making the pages look just right have meant so much. Once again it has been a rewarding synergy working with Stephen Piersanti on the analytique drawings that distill the important essence of each project.

A special thanks to Bunny Williams for her thoughtful and heartfelt Foreword. I still remember our first residential project as if it were yesterday. Your mentoring helped me immeasurably in the early years.

With profound gratitude, I wish to thank my writer and the love of my life, Elizabeth Heilman Brooke Murray, for her skillful crafting of the chapters and bringing these projects to life in words.

Since I believe it all comes back to family, I wish to thank Gabe, Luke, Jesse, James, Will and Alex for their support and understanding.

I will forever be grateful to Albert Hadley. His confidence in me launched the beginnings of the work here exhibited.

First published in 2018 by The Monacelli Press.
All rights reserved.

Library of Congress Control Number 2018945392
ISBN 978158093-503-6

Captions
Page 2: This new stair opening connects two prewar apartments in New York City's Majestic. The Greek key balustrade cast in nickel silver perfectly aligns with each machined fluted picket.
Page 4: Custom bookshelves and a daybed with trundle bed beneath are key program elements that allow a sitting room to double as a guest room.
Page 6: In a library, custom millwork frames books and precious collections.
Page 8: Favorite bucolic scenes of Central Park were captured on a commissioned mural by Scott Waterman that wraps around the gallery and connects the two floors of this new duplex.
Page 11: Thanks to a pair of pocket doors, this cerused oak sitting room complements the master bedroom.
Page 255 : With French doors, a new glass-and-bronze balustrade, and paving in a basket weave pattern, this terrace overlooking Central Park has become one of Manhattan's most remarkable outdoor rooms.

Photography Credits
Bruce Buck: 128–134
Pieter Estersohn: 11, 166–169, 172–174, 175 top right, bottom left and bottom right, 176, 177
Nick Johnson: 138–151
Francesco Lagnese: Front cover, 6, 73–87, 90–105, 109–119, 210–223
Scott Langley: 171, 175 top left
Eric Roth: 122–127, 135
Durston Saylor: 2, 4, 52–69, 120–135, 181–193, 196–207, 226–235, 239–253, back cover
Simon Upton: 8, 15–31, 255
Björn Wallander: 34–49, 154–163

Designed by Doug Turshen and Steve Turner

Printed in China

The Monacelli Press
6 West 18th Street
New York, New York 10011

www.monacellipress.com